Tastes Good!

Tastes Good!

Simple, Seasonal Recipes from a Northfield Kitchen

Columns by Jean Mohrig

Edited by Jerry Mohrig

with illustrations by Pat Lampe

BLACK
WILLOW
PRESS

Published by Black Willow Press, Northfield, MN.

ISBN: 0-939394-14-6

Cover and interior design by Mark F. Heiman.

Printed in the United States of America.

Contents

"Main Street U.S.A." P. Lampe 1976

Cakes, Pies & Tarts

Celebrations & Festivals

Cookies & Bars

Desserts

Hors d'Oeuvres

Meats

Miscellaneous

Pancakes

Soups

Vegetables

Introduction

Jean Mohrig wrote her creative food column, "Tastes Good," for the *Northfield News* from 1980 to 1986. She was a widely respected cook, whose kitchen produced delicious and nutritious food. Her weekly column was one of the more popular *News* features during the 1980s, and its recipes delivered what they promised. "Tastes Good" featured recipes that are fairly easy to prepare, for people who haven't spent a lot of time in the kitchen, but who like good food, especially food made simply from fresh, locally-available ingredients.

Jean believed that food should not only taste good, but that it was important in bringing people together, both the family and the community. In her first "Tastes Good" column she wrote:

> Food can be many things besides a necessity for life. It can be a celebration, a work of art, a tradition or an experiment. It can be soothing or exciting, warming or refreshing. In this column I will share some of my favorite recipes and ideas about food with you.

But "Tastes Good" columns were more than good recipes. The introductory comments in each column almost always had a personal touch, and they were filled with wit and wisdom. The introductions reflected Jean's sense of humor, her imagination, and her empathy. They were also rooted in the seasons of the year and the seasons of our lives.

It was in her mother's kitchen that Jean began her love affair with food; they cooked together regularly during the years she was growing up. After graduating from Carleton College, Jean married a man who liked to eat and was willing to try most everything that she cooked. Jean and Jerry raised three children who also liked to eat; the children often cooked with her, and the family ate the evening meal together virtually every day. Jean used and developed recipes which led to good, but not necessarily fancy, food. Invitations to her dinner parties were seldom turned down. Travels and extensive reading led to new and more exotic perspectives. In 1984 Jean traced the development of the column:

When I brashly offered to write this column for the *News* four years ago, I thought it would be an easy way to compile a cookbook of family recipes for each of my children. But since I couldn't just send in a list of recipes, I began by accompanying each recipe with a paragraph telling why I had chosen it. The lead paragraph soon branched out to discuss ingredients, explain techniques, or even comment on what was happening in my family.

As the years have passed, I have compiled my cookbooks, and the scope of the recipes has grown from just family favorites to recipes I have made and adapted, which I think others would enjoy even though some family members do not consider them favorites.

I have also had an unexpected bonus in writing the column—friendship. I have enjoyed people coming up to me and saying, "You don't know me, but I read your column...," the telephone calls from people saying thank you for a recipe or asking for help in the midst of a kitchen catastrophe, and the cards which begin, "I feel that I know you."

When Jean ended her column in 1986, the *News* reported: "Our reader surveys always found her column well-read, and after reading many other recipe columns, we felt hers was the best in the state."

After Jean's sudden death in 1999, Jerry decided to publish the best of her columns so that others could continue to enjoy them. Most "Tastes Good" columns were written before the computer age, so the scanning and editing process took some time, but revisions were kept to a minimum so that the columns would retain Jean's touch. An editorial committee chose some 170 columns for this book, out of the over 300 that were originally published in the *Northfield News*. The committee was composed of local residents Patricia Lampe, Ruth Anna Miller, Joan Reitz, and Jerry Mohrig, and it benefited from long-distance advice from Sara Mohrig Carney. We thank the *Northfield News* for giving its approval to our project and the editorial committee for its good work, which everyone seemed to enjoy.

The Mohrig Family
Jerry, David, and Sara
Northfield, Minnesota

Breads

Bridge Square

Phampe

A FRIEND RECENTLY ASKED me about a recipe which called for three pounds of zucchini. How many zucchini make three pounds? Further conversation brought out the fact that she was going to make a soup, so I told her that the amount of zucchini didn't have to be exact even if she was following a recipe, so long as the amount of zucchini was right to her taste.

This points out a problem that arises quite often in the kitchen. You have a recipe you want to try, but perhaps you don't have one of the ingredients, or you know you don't like one of the ingredients.

Don't be afraid to substitute or even omit ingredients. This is particularly easy to do with things like soups, stews and vegetable dishes that have a fairly high liquid content. Also don't be afraid to taste as you cook. Remember you are making something that should taste good to you. This takes a bit of confidence, but not much. If you start out with good ingredients, it is hard to produce something which is inedible.

There is also a time to follow a recipe closely. When you are making something in which texture is important (baked goods, candy, jelly, puddings), changing an ingredient can have a great effect on the finished product, and substitutions should be approached more cautiously. Flavorings can usually be easily altered, but major ingredients should be used as specified in the recipe. However, sometimes it is fun to experiment and make wild substitutions. Just don't plan on being able to serve the results to company.

I have always picked my zucchini when young and tender and then had to worry about pressing out as much liquid as possible so the batter would not be too wet, but when I worked on this recipe, I had a monstrous zucchini squash. I removed the seeds before grating it and ended up with a bowl of crisp dry shreds which made some of the best zucchini bread I have ever tasted.

Zucchini Bread

3 eggs
1 cup vegetable oil
2 teaspoons vanilla
2 cups sugar
3 cups flour
1 teaspoon salt
1 teaspoon baking soda
1 teaspoon baking powder
1 teaspoon cinnamon
2 ¼ cups finely-grated, unpeeled zucchini with excess moisture pressed out
1 cup chopped nuts (optional)

Combine the eggs, oil and vanilla in a blender container. Blend until foamy. Slowly add the sugar with the blender running and blend until fluffy. Sift or stir the flour, salt, baking soda, baking powder and cinnamon into a mixing bowl. Add the egg mixture to these dry ingredients and stir until mixed. Stir in the zucchini and nuts. Divide the batter between three small (7 ⅜ inch) greased loaf pans and bake in a preheated 350° oven for one hour or until done. The zucchini bread freezes well.

I THINK THAT THE SMELL of baking bread is one of the best smells there is. It will always remind me of my mother, and I hope that someday it will provide pleasant memories for my children too.

My mother is an old-fashioned bread maker—no measurements—and her bread is consistently delicious. I'm more comfortable with a recipe in front of me, even if I don't follow it exactly.

Much has been written lately about the mystique of bread making. There are whole books devoted to the subject and almost every cook book has a section on the techniques involved. Don't be scared off by all the verbiage. Roll up your sleeves and try it. As long as your yeast bubbles after you have dissolved it in warm water, you will undoubtedly produce something better than anything you can buy. I like to use the cake yeast from the refrigerator case at the grocery store if possible. I think it tries harder than the granulated kind. But if you don't bake often, granulated yeast stores better and works fine, although the dough may take a little longer to rise. I also prefer unbleached flour and usually add about a half cup of wheat germ to the dough.

Jonathan's Favorite Rolls

1 package dry yeast
¼ cup sugar
½ teaspoon salt
¾ cup warm water (About 110°)
2 ¼ cups flour
1 egg
¼ cup butter or margarine

Dissolve the yeast, sugar and salt in the warm water in a large bowl. Stir in one cup of flour and beat vigorously for two minutes. Add the egg and butter, beating well after each addition. Stir in the remaining flour and beat for a minute. Cover the bowl with plastic wrap and set in a warm place to rise until doubled in bulk, about one hour. Stir down and divide the dough between greased cupcake pans. Let the dough rise again, about 45 minutes. Bake in a preheated 400° oven for approximately 15 minutes. Makes 12 rolls. Leftovers may be split and toasted.

LAST WEEK WHEN I was looking through my recipes for batter breads, I came across recipes for homemade English muffins and crumpets. They are both very good, but even Julia Child admits that they are long on snob appeal because there are such excellent commercial versions available.

They also take a fair amount of time to make and are apt to make your kitchen look like a disaster area before you are finished with the project.

It is much easier to make a loaf of English muffin bread. When sliced about a half inch thick and well buttered, it is an excellent breakfast bread. It also makes a good base for hot, open-face sandwiches such as broiled cheese or bacon and tomato.

This loaf is much more moist than its commercial bakery brother.

English Muffin Bread

1 package dry yeast
1 tablespoon sugar
½ cup warm water (about 110°)
2 ½ cups flour
2 teaspoons salt
1 cup warm milk
¼ teaspoon soda dissolved in 1 tablespoon warm water

Combine the yeast, sugar and warm water in a large bowl and stir until the yeast and sugar dissolve. Let the mixture sit until bubbles begin to form. Add the flour mixed with the salt, and the warm milk in alternate portions while stirring vigorously. Beat the dough until it shows some elasticity. Cover and let it rise in a warm place until doubled in bulk, about one to 1 ¼ hours. Stir down. Add the soda, dissolved in the warm water, and beat for about one minute, distributing the soda mixture thoroughly (if not distributed thoroughly the bread will be streaked). Turn the dough into one greased 10 inch or two 8 inch bread pans. Let it rise again in a warm place for about 1 to 1 ¼ hours and bake in a 375° oven until golden brown on top and shrunk slightly from the sides of the pan. Cool 5 minutes before removing from the pan.

HERE IS A VERY GOOD recipe for lemon bread. A thin slice of this fresh tasting bread and a cup of good tea would certainly brighten up a winter afternoon. I find that the bread is so moist and flavorful that it needs no butter to accompany it.

Lemon Bread

Bread:
1 ½ cups flour
1 teaspoon baking powder
1 cup sugar
½ teaspoon salt
2 eggs
½ cup milk
½ cup oil
1 ½ teaspoons grated lemon peel

Glaze:
4 tablespoons lemon juice
⅓ cup sugar

Place the flour, baking powder, sugar and salt in a mixing bowl and stir to mix thoroughly. Blend together the eggs, milk, oil and lemon peel. Pour the egg mixture over the flour mixture and stir until thoroughly blended. Pour the batter into a well-greased bread pan, 9×5 or 10×3 ½ inches, and bake in a preheated 350° oven for 40–45 minutes.

Meanwhile, make the glaze by mixing the sugar and lemon juice together. If the sugar does not completely dissolve in the juice, heat the mixture gently until it dissolves.

When the bread is done, remove it from the oven and immediately poke holes in the bread using a thin skewer or tooth pick. Slowly spoon the glaze over the bread. Let the bread sit in its pan for an additional ten minutes and then turn it out on a rack to cool.

I recently rediscovered an old favorite of mine – date-nut bread. I had forgotten how good this dark, heavy, moist quick bread tastes. Here is my mother's recipe for this delicious bread, chock-full of dates and nuts.

Date-Nut Bread

4 ounces dates
¾ cup boiling water
1 tablespoon butter
1 egg, well beaten
1 ½ cups sugar
2 ¾ cups flour
2 teaspoons baking soda
½ teaspoon baking powder
1 teaspoon vanilla
¾ cup chopped nut meats
¾ cup cold water

Cut the dates into small pieces and place them in a large mixing bowl. Pour the boiling water over the dates and add the butter. Allow this mixture to stand until it is close to room temperature; then add the egg, stirring well. Sift or stir together the sugar, flour, baking soda, and baking powder and add this to the date mixture. Also add the vanilla and cold water. Mix well.

Pour the batter into one large bread pan which has been greased and lined with wax paper; the bread can also be baked in two small loaf pans which have been prepared in the same manner. Bake in a preheated 350° oven for 50–60 minutes. Turn the bread out on a rack to cool. Remove the waxed paper while the loaf is still warm.

One of the more subtle signs of spring is the disappearance of applesauce, peach pies, and zucchini bread from my freezer. They are my personal weapons against winter menu blahs, and I have used all my ammunition this long winter.

Since the last loaf of zucchini bread recently went to a church "picnic," I was especially glad to find "banana bread specials" available at the grocery store this week. I made a double batch of banana bread and froze it for future use. My recipe makes a rather sweet, dense, moist bread. It makes one large loaf or two small loaves (7 ¾ × 3 ⅝ × 2 ¼ inch pans). The bread keeps well. It is also very good toasted.

Banana Bread

½ cup margarine
1 cup brown sugar
2 large eggs
2 cups flour
½ teaspoon salt
½ teaspoon baking soda
1 ½ cups mashed bananas
½ cup chopped nuts (optional)

Cream the margarine and sugar together. Add the eggs and beat well. Combine the flour, salt and baking soda and stir this mixture into the creamed margarine and sugar, alternately with the mashed bananas. Fold in the nuts. Pour the batter into a well-greased large loaf pan or two small loaf pans and let stand 20 minutes at room temperature. (This allows any trapped air bubbles to escape so that the finished bread won't have "tunnels.") Bake in a preheated 350° oven for 45–60 minutes or until the loaf tests done. (If in doubt, bake an additional five minutes.) Let the bread cool five minutes before removing it from the pan. It's delicious when served warm.

ONE OF THE JOYS of autumn is lovely tart, crisp apples. No matter how much cold storage has improved, apples fresh off the tree still taste the best. After eating your fill of just plain apples, it's time to think about using them in other ways. It's time for apple pie, apple pancakes, apple crisp, apple butter and applesauce.

I like to freeze enough bright pink applesauce, made from Minjon apples, to last almost to the next year's harvest. It makes an excellent accompaniment to pork, can serve as a simple dessert when topped with a sprinkle of cinnamon, is a nutritious snack, or can be one of the ingredients in baked goods.

Applesauce-oatmeal quick bread makes a good addition to a brown bag lunch when spread with a little cream cheese and also makes a good breakfast treat when lightly toasted and topped with a little butter. It is a nice, moist bread that keeps well.

Applesauce-Oatmeal Bread

2 cups flour
1 cup oatmeal
4 teaspoons baking powder
¼ teaspoon baking soda
½ teaspoon salt
1 egg
¾ cup brown sugar, packed down
¾ cup applesauce
½ cup water
2 tablespoons (⅛ cup) oil

In a large mixing bowl stir together the flour, oatmeal, baking powder, soda and salt until they are well mixed. In another smaller bowl beat together the egg, brown sugar, applesauce, water and oil until well blended. Add the egg mixture to the flour mixture and stir until the flour is just moistened. Turn into a greased 9×5×3 loaf pan. Bake in a preheated 350° oven for one hour or until a toothpick inserted in the center comes out clean. Cool in the pan for about 10 minutes and then turn out on a rack to cool completely.

For years I have half-heartedly looked for a recipe that would duplicate our favorite cornbread. This has resulted in a small collection of recipes, neatly held together with a paper clip.

The other evening when I had a nice pot of lentil soup ready for supper, I decided that cornbread would taste good with it. I pulled out a yellowed clipping and decided to make "Mother's Cornbread." It turned out to be very good.

I baked the bread in a heavy 10 inch skillet. It could also be baked in an 8 or 9 inch square cake pan. Pouring the batter into a hot pan assures a nice bottom crust. This Southern-type cornbread would be good with almost any hearty soup, chili or the traditional chicken. Any leftovers might be eaten as dessert with a little honey, in addition to the butter which the relatively dry cornbread demands.

Mother's Cornbread

3 tablespoons butter or margarine
1 cup cornmeal
½ cup flour
2 teaspoons baking powder
½ teaspoon salt
1 tablespoon sugar
2 eggs
1 cup milk

Melt the butter in a heavy 10 inch skillet or 8 inch cake pan while the oven is being preheated to 350°. In a medium-sized bowl, combine the cornmeal, flour, baking powder, salt and sugar.

In a small bowl, beat the eggs with a fork and add the milk and about 2 tablespoons of the melted butter. Quickly stir the milk mixture into the dry ingredients and pour the batter into the hot pan. Bake 20–25 minutes in a 350° oven. Serves six to eight.

Here is a recipe for pumpkin rolls. The pumpkin adds moisture, a bit of flavor, and a smoother texture to the light, slightly-sweet whole wheat rolls. If you have had trouble baking with yeast, remember to check the temperature at which you activate the dry yeast. Yeast is alive, and if you remove it from the refrigerator and place it in water that is too warm, you may actually kill the yeast cells. Most manufacturers recommend using water at a temperature of between 105° and 115°. If you don't have a thermometer that works in this range, the water should feel barely warm to the inside of your wrist. If the water is not warm enough, it will simply take longer for your dough to rise, but it will eventually rise. If the water is too hot, no matter what else you do, the bread will be unsatisfactory.

These rolls go well with a good stew, or you might want to make some now and freeze them for Thanksgiving dinner. Canned pumpkin works fine in this recipe.

Pumpkin Whole Wheat Rolls

½ cup warm water (105–115°)
¼ cup brown sugar
2 envelopes dry active yeast
3 eggs, lightly beaten
½ cup cooked, mashed pumpkin
3 tablespoons melted butter or margarine
1 ½ cups whole wheat flour
1 ¾ cups unbleached flour
½ teaspoon salt

Mix together the water, sugar and yeast in a small bowl and let stand until foamy; this activation step will take 10–15 minutes. Add the eggs, pumpkin and butter to the yeast mixture and stir until fairly smooth.

In a large mixing bowl combine the whole wheat and unbleached flours and salt. Stir in the yeast/pumpkin mixture. The dough will be soft but not too sticky. Up to another ½ cup of unbleached flour may be added if necessary. Turn the dough out onto a lightly-floured work surface and knead it until the dough is smooth (5–10 minutes).

Place the dough in a greased bowl, cover it with a damp cloth, and let it rise in a warm (70–75°) place until doubled in bulk. This will take 30 minutes to one hour depending on the temperature of your kitchen.

Punch down the dough and cut it into 18 pieces. Roll each piece between your hands to make a smooth ball and place the rolls on a lightly-greased baking sheet, leaving about 1– 1 ½ inches between them. Cover the rolls with a damp cloth and allow them to rise again until about doubled (15–30 minutes).

Bake in a preheated 375° oven until golden brown (about 15 minutes). Remove from the oven and cool about 10 minutes before removing from the pan. The rolls may be frozen and reheated before serving if desired.

The other day I wanted to bake something that was quick and easy to make, that would call only for ingredients that I had on hand and that wouldn't disintegrate in a brown-bag lunch. Pear bread filled all of these criteria. It makes an excellent lunch treat when spread with cream cheese.

When I make it again, I think I will try adding three or four tablespoons of coarsely grated semi-sweet chocolate or perhaps a quarter of a cup of miniature chocolate chips in order to obtain the French taste combination of pears and chocolate. I suppose one could even try adding two tablespoons of baking cocoa to the batter in order to obtain a light chocolatey taste.

Pear Bread

2–3 fresh pears
½ cup oil
1 cup sugar
2 eggs
¼ cup sour cream
1 teaspoon vanilla
2 cups flour
½ teaspoon salt
1 teaspoon baking soda
½ teaspoon cinnamon
¼ teaspoon nutmeg
½ cup chopped walnuts

Peel, halve and core the pears; chop finely. You need one cup of chopped pear. In a large bowl, beat together the oil and sugar until very well blended. Add the eggs, one at a time, beating well after each addition. Stir in the sour cream and vanilla.

Sift or stir together the flour, salt, baking soda, cinnamon and nutmeg and add it to the sugar mixture, beating until well blended. Fold in the pears and walnuts. Spoon the batter into a well-greased and floured 9×5 loaf pan.

Bake in a preheated 350° oven for one hour or until a toothpick inserted in the center comes out clean. Cool in the pan 5–10 minutes; then remove from the pan and cool completely before slicing. Spread with butter or cream cheese, if desired.

Cakes, Pies & Tarts

St Olaf - Old Main

P Lampe

I PULLED THE FIRST rhubarb of spring last week. The leaves were a vivid full green and the stalks were thick, red and shiny. I thought winter was truly gone and spring was here.

Rhubarb has long been regarded as a spring tonic, and back in the days when fresh fruits and vegetables were unavailable during the winter months, a dish of fresh rhubarb sauce must have started up sluggish digestive systems with a bang. I know that many people still like a dish of stewed rhubarb although others prefer their rhubarb with something.

For those who prefer rhubarb in less concentrated form, here is a recipe for a simple fruit coffee cake which uses a can of pie filling. If you use a couple of cups of sliced fresh rhubarb with a can of strawberry pie filling, a fresh-tasting spring treat emerges. Remember that you can make the cake using just a can of your favorite fruit-pie filling, although it may turn out to be a good deal sweeter.

Strawberry-Rhubarb Coffee Cake

Cake:
½ cup soft butter or margarine
1 cup sugar
2 cups flour
2 teaspoons baking powder
1 egg plus milk to make 1 cup

Fruit layer:
2 cups sliced rhubarb
1 can strawberry pie filling

Topping:
⅔ cup flour
⅔ cup sugar
⅓ cup butter or margarine

Cream together the butter and sugar. Sift or stir together the flour and baking powder and add this to the butter mixture. Break the egg into a measuring cup and add enough milk to make one cup of liquid. Add this to the butter mixture as well and mix until a smooth batter is obtained. Spread the batter in a well-greased 9×13 inch pan.

Arrange the rhubarb over the top of the batter and spoon the pie filling over the rhubarb.

Make the topping by mixing the flour, sugar and butter together to form fine crumbs. Sprinkle over the top of the cake. Bake in a preheated 350° oven for 35–40 minutes.

HERE ARE TWO CAKE recipes where you can feature the spring bounty of rhubarb. The first is for a rhubarb cake which can be served as a coffee cake as it is. Or it can be dressed up with a drift of softly whipped cream and dusted with a bit of cinnamon for a memorable dessert. Use young, pink rhubarb if possible.

Fresh Rhubarb Cake

½ cup butter or margarine, softened
1 ½ cups brown sugar, packed
1 egg
1 teaspoon vanilla
2 cups flour
¼ teaspoon salt
1 teaspoon baking soda
1 tablespoon lemon juice
1 cup milk
2 cups rhubarb, coarsely chopped
½ cup walnuts or pecans, chopped
½ cup sugar
1 teaspoon cinnamon

In a large bowl, cream the butter until it is light. Add the brown sugar slowly, continuing to cream until the mixture is well blended and fluffy. Beat in the egg and vanilla.

Sift or stir together the flour, salt and baking soda. Stir the lemon juice into the milk. Alternately, add portions of the flour mixture and then the milk to the creamed mixture, beating only enough to blend after each addition. Gently fold in the rhubarb. Pour the batter into a well-greased and floured 9×13 pan, spreading evenly.

In a small bowl, blend together the sugar, nuts, and cinnamon and sprinkle evenly over the batter. Bake in a preheated 350° oven for 45–50 minutes or until the cake tests done. Cool in the pan for about 30 minutes before serving. Can be served warm or cold. Serves eight to ten. Freezes well.

And here is the other rhubarb dessert for you to try.

Rhubarb Crumble

3 cups sliced rhubarb
2 eggs
1 ⅜ cups white sugar
2 tablespoons flour
1 cup flour
½ cup brown sugar
1 teaspoon soda
5 tablespoons butter or margarine

Grease a 9×13 pan and spread the rhubarb evenly over the bottom. In a medium-sized bowl, beat the eggs. Add the white sugar and the two tablespoons of flour and beat well. Pour this mixture over the rhubarb. You may use the same bowl to mix together the one cup of flour, brown sugar, soda and butter and make a crumbly mixture. Sprinkle this over the top of the dessert. Bake in a preheated 350° oven for 45 minutes. Serve either warm or cold. Serves ten.

RECENTLY WE WENT CHERRY picking in Wisconsin's Door County. We picked ten buckets of sour cherries and then took them back to our friends' home in Ephraim and pitted them all. As we sat on their screened porch working happily together, it occurred to me that we very seldom sit together and work with our hands anymore. Gone are the days when families sat together to snap beans or peel peaches for canning.

Machines and the vast array of processed foods that are available in the supermarkets have made such gatherings unnecessary. Perhaps, in the bustle of modern life there really isn't enough time for such labor intensive gatherings, which is a shame because we had fun. We visited together, catching up on the comings and goings of various members of our families, joked about the difficulty of scratching your nose when your hands are sticky with cherry juice and were surprised at how quickly the job got done and the cherries were ready for the freezer. We had a good time.

At breakfast our hosts served a delicious light cherry coffee cake, whose recipe comes from one of Ephraim's old hotels. The recipe calls for cherries, but I think that a cup of blueberries or chopped peaches would also be good. The fruit should be well drained.

Quick Coffee Cake

Cake:
½ cup butter or margarine
1 cup sugar
2 eggs, separated
¼ teaspoon salt
1 teaspoon baking powder
1 ½ cups flour
½ cup milk
1 cup fruit (optional)

Topping:
6 tablespoons flour
¼ cup brown sugar
2 tablespoons butter or margarine
½ teaspoon baking powder

Cream together the butter and sugar. Add the egg yolks and beat well. Sift or stir together the salt, baking powder and flour. If you are adding fruit, stir it into the flour mixture. Alternately add the flour mixture and the milk to the sugar-egg yolk mixture. Beat the egg whites until they are stiff and fold them into the batter.

Place the batter in a greased and floured 9 inch square pan and sprinkle with the topping made by blending together the flour, brown sugar, butter and baking powder. Bake in a preheated 350° oven for 30 minutes. Serves six to eight.

MORNING COFFEE WITH FRIENDS is a tradition that seems to me to be worth preserving. It's so easy to get too busy – whether it is because of employment, a combination of family and community pressures or just a sense of not having enough time – so easy to become trapped in our own worlds, so easy to forget the pleasure which comes with sharing and the comfort that comes with just being together with friends. Perhaps we need someone to declare a Coffee Month. Or perhaps we could celebrate our own personal time of touching base with friends, of becoming reacquainted with them and with ourselves, even if it has to be done on Friday evening, Saturday morning or Sunday afternoon.

This is a recipe I got from my mother years ago. It produces a coffee cake which freezes extremely well. My mother cut it into quarters before freezing so that she always had something ready when friends dropped in for a cup of coffee. A good Swede never serves a naked cup of coffee.

Sour Cream Coffee Cake

1 cup margarine
1 ¼ cup sugar
2 eggs
1 cup sour cream
1 teaspoon vanilla
2 cups flour
1 teaspoon baking powder
½ teaspoon baking soda
½ cup finely chopped nuts
2 tablespoons sugar
1 teaspoon cinnamon

Cream the margarine and 1 ¼ cups sugar together. Add the eggs and beat well. Stir in the sour cream and vanilla. Sift or stir together the flour, baking powder and soda, and add to the sour cream mixture; mix well. In a small bowl, stir together the nuts, sugar and cinnamon.

Place one half of the dough in a greased tube pan, sprinkle with half of the nut mixture, add the rest of dough and top with the remaining nut mixture. Bake in a preheated 350° oven for 45 minutes.

Here is the recipe for almond cake, another cake that goes very well with a cup of coffee.

Almond Cake

3 eggs, separated
½ cup butter or margarine
1 cup sugar
1 teaspoon almond extract
½ cup milk
1 ⅓ cups flour
1 ½ teaspoons baking powder
Confectioner's sugar

Beat the egg whites until stiff peaks form, and then set them aside. Cream the butter, sugar, egg yolks, and almond extract and then gradually beat in the milk. Combine the flour and baking powder and stir it into the creamed mixture. Carefully fold in the egg whites just until they are blended.

Pour into a greased and floured 9 inch square pan or 10 inch round skillet. Bake in a preheated 350° oven until done (30 to 35 minutes). Let the cake cool in the pan for 10 minutes and then invert it onto a serving plate. Cool and dust with confectioner's sugar. Serves eight to ten.

IT WAS DIFFICULT TO say that final farewell to my husband's mother even though we knew she was at peace, no longer frustrated at having been robbed by a stroke of her speech and much of her ability to move. Her roots ran deep in Grand Rapids, Michigan. She lived there her whole life. At the funeral home, we talked to a woman whom she had helped over the daily hurdle of going off to kindergarten when they were both five. The cemetery was ablaze with autumn color when she was placed next to her husband, who had died twenty-two years ago, and a young son who had died over fifty years ago.

Blanche Mohrig was a small, white-haired woman with a twinkle in her eye. She enjoyed a good joke even when it turned out to be on her. We would kid her about her card games with "the girls," none of whom would ever be seventy again. Most of all, she enjoyed her family. She was always ready for a picnic, a meal out, a trip out to the lake or just a visit over the telephone. Even though she often said, "I don't know if I'll live to see…", she didn't give up and lived to see all the graduations, marriages, anniversaries, baptisms and birthdays that are part of being a member of an extended family. She had fun for almost 87 years and left behind many pleasant memories.

She was a thrifty woman, who remembered well the hard lessons the great depression had taught her, and she was a good neighbor. If someone were sick or in need in any way, there was a pot of vegetable soup or a coffee cake to share. A time of celebration called for sending a lemon pie. In her last years these kindnesses were repaid by the neighbors who shopped for her, mowed her lawn or shoveled her snow.

Here is her recipe for lemon cake pie, which is a lemon custard pie topped with a layer of light, lemony, sponge-type cake.

Lemon Pie Cake

1 unbaked pie crust
5 tablespoons flour
1 cup sugar
2 egg yolks
2 tablespoons melted butter
Grated rind and juice of 1 lemon
1 cup milk
2 egg whites, stiffly beaten

In a large bowl beat together the flour, sugar, egg yolks, melted butter, lemon juice and rind. Stir in the milk and continue beating for about three minutes.

Fold about a quarter of the lemon mixture into the stiffly beaten egg whites and then fold this egg white mixture back into the lemon mixture. Pour into an unbaked 8 or 9 inch pie crust and bake for 40 minutes in a preheated 350° oven. Serves six to eight people.

Not only does cooler weather bring on a desire for heartier fare, such as meat based soups and stews, it also seems to trigger the chocolate munchies at my house. I don't know if this is because our bodies need a few more calories as they are adjusting to the temperature change or that chocolate doesn't seem to be a summer taste unless it is combined with ice cream.

Here is a recipe that can partially satisfy those chocolate longings while also serving as a welcome addition to brown bag lunches, which may also be part of the autumn scene at your house. These chocolatey cupcakes may be baked plain, topped with chopped nuts, or if you are trying to get all the nutrition possible even in rich desserts, topped with a sprinkling of granola. I haven't tried it, but granola could possibly also be substituted for the nuts in the batter.

If you prefer a dense fudge-like consistency, bake the cupcakes only 20–23 minutes. If you prefer a more cake-like consistency, bake them 25–30 minutes. No matter how long you bake them, they will probably settle slightly as they cool.

Brownie Cupcakes

4 ounces unsweetened baking chocolate
1 cup (½ pound) butter or margarine
2 cups sugar
4 large eggs
1 teaspoon vanilla
1 cup flour
1 cup chopped nuts
⅓ cup chopped nuts

Place the chocolate and butter in a large heavy saucepan and stir constantly over low-medium heat until they are melted. Remove from the heat and stir in the sugar. Add the eggs and vanilla and beat to mix thoroughly. Stir in the flour and then 1 cup of chopped nuts.

Spoon the batter into paper-lined muffin cups, filling each one about ⅔ full. Top each cupcake with about a teaspoonful of chopped nuts. Bake in a preheated 350° oven for 20–30 minutes; the tops will be firm, but the interiors will remain moist. Let the cupcakes cool about 15 minutes before removing the muffin cups from the pan. Cool thoroughly before serving. Makes eighteen.

A FEW DAYS AGO, my eleven-year-old daughter, Sara, baked a classic American cake for my birthday and took it down to The News office. When I was asked if I planned to review it for my column, I thought why not. So, here goes:

The three-layered yellow cake was fine crumbed, quite moist and had a good vanilla flavor. The filling between the layers, which was made with thickened frozen strawberries, provided a nice contrast in flavors, as it was not too sweet. The filling also provided a pleasing visual contrast.

The frosting was creamy and good tasting. If the cake could have been refrigerated for a short period of time before serving, the frosting would have been firmer and the cake a little easier to serve. Overall, it was a most creditable attempt at a non-mix cake.

1-2-3-4 Cake

1 cup butter (or margarine)
2 cups sugar
4 eggs
3 cups sifted cake flour
½ teaspoon salt
4 teaspoons baking powder
1 cup milk
1½ teaspoons vanilla

Cream the butter and then cream in the sugar until fluffy. Beat in the eggs using the highest speed of your mixer. Sift or stir the flour with the baking powder and salt. Turn off the mixer and add the flour mixture. Then turn on the mixer to its lowest speed and add the milk and vanilla. When smooth, pour the batter into three 8 or 9 inch greased cake pans. Bake in a preheated 350° oven for about 25 minutes or until the cake springs back when touched lightly with a fingertip. Cool a few minutes before removing the cake from the pans and placing on a rack to cool thoroughly before frosting.

Whipped Frosting

3 tablespoons flour
1 cup milk
½ cup butter or margarine
½ cup shortening
1 cup granulated sugar
1 teaspoon vanilla

Combine the flour and milk in a small saucepan and cook together until very thick. Cool. Cream the butter or margarine together with the shortening. Add sugar and beat until smooth and fluffy. Add the cooled flour-milk mixture and beat until smooth. Add the vanilla and mix thoroughly. The recipe makes enough frosting for the top and sides of a large cake.

The Northfield Public Library has more than one thousand entries in the online catalog under "Cookery." On the shelves in the 641 section are books such as *The Fannie Farmer Cookbook*, Julia Child's classics on French cookery, and many ethnic cookbooks including the recipe books from the Time-Life international cooking series. In addition, the library subscribes to *Gourmet* and *Bon Appetit* magazines, with files going back for two years.

With a little detective work, the answer to just about any question you might have about cooking is probably available on the shelves of the library. The various books can also provide inspiration to try new recipes or modify old favorites for a change of pace.

When visiting the library, don't forget to look also in the oversized book section where the books with large-sized pages are kept. If you are looking for a particular title and the library does not have it, it can probably be obtained through an interlibrary loan.

Here is a favorite recipe which will please chocolate fans.

Fudge Pudding Cake

Cake:
2 tablespoons soft butter
¾ cup sugar
1 cup flour
1 ½ teaspoons baking powder
2 tablespoons cocoa
½ cup milk

Topping:
½ cup chopped nuts (optional)
½ cup sugar
½ cup firmly packed brown sugar
½ cup cocoa
1 ¼ cups boiling water

Cake: Lightly cream the butter and sugar together. Sift or stir together the flour, baking powder and cocoa and add it to the butter mixture, along with the milk. Beat until well mixed. Turn the batter into a greased 9 inch square pan.

Topping: Sprinkle the batter with nuts then with the white and brown sugars and cocoa, which have been mixed together. Gently pour the boiling water over the top of the batter.

Bake in a preheated 350° oven for about 40 minutes or until the cake leaves the sides of the pan and the center is springy to the touch. Let the cake cool slightly before serving; it is also good cold. It may be topped with whipped cream or ice cream. Makes six to eight servings.

I DEBATED AS TO whether the general public is ready for this traditional family birthday cake. Let me warn you, it is only for the chocolate lovers among us. It also isn't for those who like their cakes light and delicate. But if what you really like is a good substantial chocolatey chocolate cake, this could become your favorite too.

My mother-in-law gave me this recipe shortly after I married. She had copied it down in a high-school home economics class many years ago. Her name for it was "crazy chocolate cake," but in our family it became affectionately known as "ton cake."

The recipe can easily be cut in half and baked in an 8 inch square pan. It is always topped with seven minute frosting.

Crazy Chocolate Cake

2 cups sugar
2 eggs
1 cup buttermilk
1 cup cocoa
1 cup shortening
2 teaspoons soda
1 teaspoon salt
2 teaspoons vanilla
3 cups flour
1 cup boiling water

Place all the ingredients, in the order given, in a large bowl and beat for three minutes, scraping down the sides of the bowl occasionally. Place the batter in a well-greased 9×13 pan and bake in a preheated 350° oven for 40 to 45 minutes, or until the cake begins to pull away from the sides of the pan. Cool thoroughly before frosting.

Seven Minute Frosting

2 egg whites
1 ½ cups sugar
¼ teaspoon cream of tartar
1 ½ teaspoons light corn syrup (optional)
⅓ cup cold water
Dash of salt
1 teaspoon vanilla

Place all of the ingredients except the vanilla in the top of a double boiler. Beat to mix well with an electric beater. Place the pan over boiling water and beat constantly until the mixture forms peaks, about seven minutes. Remove from the heat, add the vanilla and continue beating until the frosting reaches spreading consistency. This amount will frost the top and sides of two 9 inch layers, one 10 inch tube cake, 24 cup cakes or the top of a 9×13 cake very generously.

THE ITALIAN PRUNE PLUMS which are now available at the produce counter remind me of the little German village we lived in. Almost every yard had its plum tree. The plums were converted into preserves and delicious Pflaum Kuchen. As you walked down the street, the air was filled with the smell of the ripening fruit and hum of the wasps which were feasting on the windfalls.

Did you know that the reason Bavarian beer steins have lids is to keep wasps out of the beer? Otherwise, a wasp might bite you in the mouth or throat and the resultant swelling could be fatal. For the same reason, soft drinks are not drunk directly from the can but only from a clear glass.

Plum Cake

Cake:
1 ¼ cups flour
½ teaspoon salt
2 teaspoons sugar
1 teaspoon baking powder
½ cup butter or margarine
1 egg yolk
2–3 tablespoons milk
15–20 Italian plums

Topping:
¾ cup sugar
1 ½ tablespoons flour
2 tablespoons butter or margarine
¼ teaspoon cinnamon

Cake: Stir together the flour, salt, sugar and baking powder. With a fork, blend in the butter and then stir in the egg yolk and milk to make a crumbly dough. With your fingers, press the dough into the bottom and up the sides of a buttered 9 inch round pan.

Cut the plums in half from top to bottom and remove their pits. Place the plums side by side, cut side up, completely covering the batter.

Topping: Make the topping by mixing all the ingredients together with your fingers. Sprinkle over the plums, covering well up to the edges. Bake for 30–35 minutes in a preheated 375° oven. Serve warm or cold.

ONE OF MY ALL-TIME favorite billboards no longer stands just north of the 35W-Northfield intersection. There was a picture of a large glass of milk with the head of a black and white cow in the lower right-hand corner. The words coming from the cow's mouth simply said, "It makes you proud to be a cow." The sign always made me smile and reflect on how lucky we are to have cows.

Milk has always been an important food item in our family, and there is always cheese in our refrigerator as well. My husband, in particular, agrees with Clifton Fadiman that "Cheese is milk's leap toward immortality." All this leads up to a reminder that June is National Dairy Month. So celebrate the cow and all that she gives us. Since it is impractical to take a cow to lunch, why not bake your favorite cheesecake, serve it up with glasses of ice-cold milk, and consider your blessings.

If you don't have a favorite cheesecake, here is a recipe for a baked New York-style cake. It follows the European tradition and has a cookie-like crust instead of one made with Graham cracker crumbs. It is made with easily obtainable cream cheese, which is somewhat richer than the pot cheese or quark which the Europeans use. Since strawberries are in such good supply right now, you might want to top each serving with some slightly-sweetened sliced berries. I think this is preferable to topping the cake with whole berries and glazing it with melted jelly, especially as the cake isn't going to be consumed in one sitting; it is also much easier. A piece of well-wrapped cheese cake will last over a week in the refrigerator, if it is well hidden. And as Sara Lee has proved so well, cheesecake does freeze well.

New York Style Cheesecake

Crust:
1 cup flour
¼ cup sugar
1 teaspoon grated lemon rind
⅔ cup butter or margarine, cut in small pieces
1 egg yolk
¼ teaspoon vanilla

Filling:
5 (8 ounce) packages cream cheese, softened
1 ¾ cups sugar
3 tablespoons flour
5 eggs
2 egg yolks
1 ½ teaspoons grated orange rind
1 ½ teaspoons grated lemon rind
1 teaspoon vanilla
¼ cup cream or whole milk

Crust: Stir together the flour, sugar and lemon rind in a medium-sized bowl. Add the butter, egg yolk and vanilla, and work to form a smooth dough; then chill the dough about one hour. Grease the bottom and sides of a 9 inch springform pan. Press about one third of the dough into a smooth layer on the bottom of the pan and bake it in a preheated 400° oven for 10 minutes.

Remove the pan from the oven and cool it well. Press the remaining dough into an even layer about two inches high on the sides of the pan. Increase the oven temperature to 475°.

Filling: In a large bowl, beat the softened cream cheese, sugar and flour until smooth. Beat in the eggs and egg yolks one at a time, beating well after each addition. Mix in the grated orange and lemon rind, vanilla and cream. Pour the batter into the prepared pan. Bake for 10 minutes in a preheated 475° oven. Then lower the oven thermostat to 200° and bake one hour. Turn off the oven, and leave the cake in the unopened oven for an additional hour; the cake will puff up and then gradually become level. Open the oven door and allow the cake to sit an additional 30 minutes. Remove the cake from the oven and remove the sides of the pan. Cool to room temperature and then refrigerate until serving time. Serves at least twelve.

THE SMELL OF SOMETHING fresh out of the oven can trigger positive mental images and feelings, which don't even have to be based on the reality of our experience. They may be based on the way things should be: kitchens should smell good; a fresh-baked cake is a way of saying, "I love you;" we all need chocolate-chip cookies at some time in our lives; not only does it smell divine and taste good, but it is good for you; it reminds me of home. Here is the recipe for my father's favorite cake. Its origins are lost in the sands of family tradition. It is not too chocolatey and has a cooked topping containing raisins, coconut and nuts. I hope you enjoy it as much as he does.

Father's Favorite Cake

Cake:
½ cup shortening
2 cups sugar
3 eggs
1 teaspoon baking soda
½ cup milk
2 ½ cups flour
3 tablespoons baking cocoa
1 teaspoon salt
1 cup boiling water

Cream together the shortening and the sugar. Add the eggs and beat well. Dissolve the baking soda in the milk and stir this into the egg mixture. Sift or stir together the flour, cocoa and salt and add it to the egg mixture, beating well. Add the boiling water and mix thoroughly.

Pour the batter into a well-greased 9×13 pan and bake in a preheated 350° oven for 40 to 45 minutes or until the cake begins to pull away from the sides of the pan.

Topping:
3 egg yolks
⅔ cup sugar
½ cup butter or margarine
½ cup white raisins
½ cup chopped nuts
½ cup coconut

In a small, heavy saucepan, beat together the egg yolks and sugar until the mixture is thick and lemon colored. Add the butter and the raisins and cook over a medium heat until thick. Stir in the nuts and coconut and spread the topping over the hot cake. Serves sixteen.

There are many types of pastry which can be used as pie crust. The simplest is made by cutting or rubbing shortening into flour to which a little salt has been added; then just enough water is added to make the dough hold together. This is the way our grandmothers made pies.

Pies used to be a staple in many family diets. Hearty meat pies were served for supper. Smaller pies or pastries found their way into lunch buckets. During the winter, pies made of apples or dried fruits and berries were the most common way of eating fruit, with a wedge of pie often appearing on the breakfast table.

Since most of us no longer need the calories provided by a hefty wedge of pie, it has become something most of us make only for a special dessert. The pastry we use has become lighter, and we roll it thinner. Since making pie isn't an everyday occurrence, it is nice to have a crust recipe to rely on. I have found that vegetable shortening makes the flakiest crust; a little bit of sugar helps the crust to brown nicely, and the addition of an egg seems to make the dough easier to handle.

Trouble Free Pie Crust

4 cups flour
1 tablespoon sugar
2 teaspoons salt
1 ¾ cups vegetable shortening (not lard, butter, margarine or oil)
½ cup water
1 tablespoon vinegar or lemon juice
1 large egg

In a large bowl, mix the flour, salt and sugar together with a fork. Add the shortening and mix with a fork until crumbly. In a small bowl, beat together the egg, water and vinegar, and add this to the flour mixture and stir until the dough holds together. Chill before rolling out. This recipe makes enough dough for two double crust pies and one single crust pie or five single crust pies. Dough can be refrigerated for a week or frozen in crust-size pieces.

For a baked pie shell, prick the dough thoroughly with a fork both on the bottom and up the sides. Then bake it in a preheated 450° oven for about 12 minutes. The very hot oven will set the dough and help prevent it from shrinking. For filled pies, follow the specific directions that come with the filling or bake at 400° for 15 minutes to brown the crust and then lower the temperature to 350° and bake for an additional 45 minutes or until done.

IN THE FOURTEENTH CENTURY, monks brought rhubarb to Europe from its native northern Asia. They cultivated it as a medicinal plant. After a long winter, when little fresh fruit or even vegetables were available, the first rhubarb of the season was undoubtedly a powerful cathartic. Poultices made from the leaves, which have a high oxalic acid content, were probably used to treat warts and corns.

The roots of this plant were carried to the New World, and pioneers took it across the country with them. It continued to be considered a spring tonic, but also found new uses as its pioneer name, pie plant, testifies. People ate it because they liked its fresh astringent taste, whether it was stewed as a pudding, cooked into a jam or conserve, or tucked between the crusts of a pie.

As transportation and better preservation methods made fruits and vegetables more readily available during the winter, rhubarb fell from favor. Cookbooks in the late 1800s paid scant attention to it. The renewed interest in natural foods has reversed this notion, and rhubarb now even appears on the supermarket produce counter and in the frozen food section. Rhubarb can easily be frozen by thinly slicing clean, dry stalks, placing a single layer of pieces on a cookie sheet so that they will freeze quickly, and then bagging the frozen rhubarb for storage.

Rhubarb cream pie is one of my favorite spring desserts. Even people who say they don't like rhubarb seem to like this pie.

Rhubarb Cream Pie

3 cups sliced rhubarb
1½ cups sugar
3 tablespoons flour
½ teaspoon nutmeg
1 tablespoon butter or margarine
2 beaten eggs
1 single 9 inch pie crust

Place the rhubarb in a pastry-lined pie pan. Blend the sugar, flour, nutmeg and butter in a small bowl. Add the eggs and mix until smooth. Pour over the rhubarb. Bake for 10 minutes in a preheated 450° oven and then reduce the oven thermostat setting to 350° and bake an additional 30 to 40 minutes.

Rhubarb muffins might make a good Sunday breakfast treat. They also go well with fried chicken. Dice the rhubarb so that the pieces are about the size of blueberries. If you have them, each muffin can be garnished with a half of a small strawberry.

Rhubarb Muffins

1 ¾ cups flour
½ cup sugar
2 ½ teaspoons baking powder
1 egg
¾ cup milk
⅓ cup vegetable oil
1 cup diced rhubarb
6 small strawberries, cut in half (optional)
Sugar

Mix the flour, sugar, and baking powder in a large bowl. Combine the egg, milk and oil in a small bowl, mixing well. Stir the liquid into the flour mixture just until moistened. Fold in the diced rhubarb. Divide the batter between 12 well-greased or paper-lined muffin tins. If using strawberries, press a strawberry half gently into the top of each muffin. Sprinkle their tops generously with sugar. Bake in a preheated 400° oven for 20 to 25 minutes.

Last fall when I was about to bake my first apple pie, I decided to check a recipe before embarking on the project since the pie was for a planned potluck dinner and not just for home consumption. My favorite cookbooks let me down.

There were all sorts of apple recipes, including one for apple custard pie or red hot apple pie, but none for just a plain old-fashioned, two-crust apple pie. Finally, I checked out my old Fannie Farmer cookbook and found a recipe there.

It turned out that the recipe was exactly how I would have proceeded on my own, so I had wasted a bit of time looking for a written recipe. But my curiosity was aroused. Whenever I looked at a new cookbook, I checked the index for apple pie. This exercise was in vain until I came across James Beard's excellent *American Cookery*. He explained that many cookbooks don't bother with a recipe because it is assumed that everyone has his own favorite recipe for this common American treat.

Since last fall I have baked many apple pies, experimenting a little each time. I don't claim to have the ultimate apple pie recipe, but I thought perhaps someone else might have looked in vain for a recipe to use as a starting point in creating this naturalized American classic (apple pie is of British origin).

If you are curious as to why I had never made an apple pie, it is because I grew up in a family where my father held firmly to the tenet that cherries made better apple pie than apples, and I married a man who added the corollary that the best apple pies are made with peaches. I should add that I do have a son who appreciates apple pie on its own merits.

Apple Pie

6 cups peeled, cored, and thinly-sliced tart apples
½ to ¾ cup sugar (to taste)
1 teaspoon cinnamon
2 tablespoons flour
A few gratings of nutmeg (optional)
¼ teaspoon salt
3 tablespoons butter
Pastry for a two-crust, 9 inch pie

Combine the apples with the sugar, spices, salt and flour and turn into a 9 inch pie plate lined with pastry. Dot the apples with butter and cover with the top crust. Crimp the edges and cut several slits in the top. Bake in a preheated 450° oven for 15 minutes. Reduce the temperature to 350° and bake 20 to 35 minutes longer. The length of time will depend on the type of apples used.

Serve topped with sharp cheddar cheese, ice cream or just as is.

Another naturalized American dessert is apple crisp, which is of German origin. This version uses oatmeal in the topping.

Apple Crisp

8 cups peeled, cored and thinly-sliced apples
1 ½ cups granulated sugar
¼ cup flour
1 cup brown sugar
1 cup oatmeal
1 cup flour
1 cup melted butter or margarine

Mix the apples, granulated sugar and ¼ cup flour together and spread in a 9×13 inch cake pan. Blend the remaining ingredients together until crumbly. Sprinkle them over the apple mixture. Bake in a preheated 350° oven for 45 minutes or until golden brown. Makes twelve servings.

This year I've decided to celebrate National Apple Month by sharing a very old apple pie recipe. Apples are one of the immigrants to this country which have been so thoroughly assimilated that we tend to think of them as being a native fruit. The first orchards here were planted by the Pilgrims in the early 1620s. Their fruit was very different from the apples we know today. It was seedy and lumpy and used mainly for making cider. But since apples do not grow true to type, the orchards soon contained many types. Favorites were propagated by grafting onto healthy root-stock and soon orchards produced a large variety. Then Johnny Appleseed gathered bags of seed from his cider mill and spread apple orchards across the American frontier.

But back to our recipe. Marlborough pie baked in a sweet, crumbly crust was very popular in the 1800s. This version is made with grated apples and produces a pie with a consistency similar to coconut cream. If you don't have any rum, you might substitute two teaspoons of vanilla; the taste will be different, but good. Cake flour, which has little gluten, is used to insure a nice crumbly consistency in the crust. If you don't have cake flour, use all-purpose flour.

Sweet Paste Pie Crust

1 cup all-purpose flour
½ cup cake flour
2 tablespoons sugar
¼ teaspoon salt
½ cup cold butter
4–6 tablespoons whipping cream
1 egg yolk

In a medium-sized bowl, mix together both flours and the sugar and salt. Cut in the butter until the mixture resembles fine crumbs. Mix 4 tablespoons of the whipping cream with the egg yolk in a small bowl and gradually stir it into the flour mixture with a fork. Stir in the remaining cream, 1 teaspoonful at a time, until the dough clings together and cleans the side of the bowl. Shape the dough into a ball, flatten it to make a 1 inch-thick circle, wrap it in plastic wrap and refrigerate for at least 3 hours. Bake as the pie recipe below directs. Makes one 9 or 10 inch crust.

Marlborough Apple Pie

Sweet paste pie crust
2 cups shredded or grated apples
½ cup raisins or currants
½ cup whipping cream
3 eggs, well beaten
⅓ cup packed brown sugar
2 tablespoons dark rum
¼ teaspoon grated nutmeg
⅛ teaspoon salt

Preheat oven to 450°. Quickly roll out the pastry on a lightly floured circle two inches larger than an inverted 9 inch pie or 10 inch tart pan. Fold the dough into quarters and ease it into the pan. Trim the overhang to 1 inch and fold the overhang in, tucking it between the crust and the pan. Press the pastry against the side of the pan to seal it. The pastry should be about ¼ inch above the edge of the pan. Prick the bottom and side of the crust with a fork. Line with aluminum foil and fill it with dried beans, rice or pie weights.

Bake on a cookie sheet until set, about eight minutes, and then remove the weights and foil. Bake until golden, about 5–10 minutes. Cool on a wire rack before filling.

Combine the apples, raisins, whipping cream, eggs, sugar, rum, nutmeg and salt in a medium-sized bowl. Pour the mixture into the prepared crust.

Bake for 15 minutes in the preheated 450° oven. Reduce the heat to 325° and bake until the filling is set, about 30 minutes. Cool on a wire rack for 15 minutes and, if using a tart pan, remove the side of the pan. Serve warm or at room temperature. Serves eight.

It seems strange to me that we celebrate the life of a third century Christian martyr by baking heart-shaped cookies and sending sentimental or funny cards to the important people in our lives, but we do. Valentine's Day seems to be one day of the year when it is a little easier for most people to say, "I love you," whether it be whispered in an ear, proclaimed on a billboard, or said with flowers, a poem, a card, or something good to eat. I can't write a poem for you, but I can share a dessert recipe which I think your loved ones will enjoy. If you don't get it made for Valentine's Day, the cherries make it appropriate to serve on Presidents' Day, or for that matter, with any winter meal when a hearty dessert would be appropriate.

The recipe calls for two cups of buttermilk biscuit mix. I usually do not use mixes, but I always have a small box of biscuit mix on the shelf. It makes a good hot biscuit when I am in a hurry or when I want a quick topping for a casserole. If you don't have the mix handy, stir together 2 cups of flour, 1 tablespoon of baking powder, ½ teaspoon of salt and cut in ¼ cup of shortening. Substitute this mixture for the mix. You should then also substitute milk for the water called for in the pie recipe.

Deep-Dish Cherry Pie

1 can (17 ounces) pitted dark sweet cherries
2 cans pitted tart red cherries
½ cup sugar
4 tablespoons cornstarch
½ teaspoon cinnamon
¼ teaspoon nutmeg
2 cups buttermilk biscuit mix
3 tablespoons sugar
¼ cup sour cream
3 tablespoons water
2 tablespoons sugar

Drain the syrup from the sweet cherries into a 2 cup measure. Drain the tart sour cherries, adding enough of their juice to the dark cherry syrup to make 2 full cups. Combine ½ cup of sugar and the cornstarch, cinnamon and nutmeg in a large saucepan. Gradually stir in the juices. Cook over medium heat, stirring constantly, until the mixture thickens and bubbles. Add the cherries and spoon into a shallow 8 cup casserole or 8 inch square pan.

Combine the biscuit mix, 3 tablespoons of sugar, the sour cream and water in a medium-sized bowl. Combine with a fork until the dough just holds together. Turn out on a floured surface and knead gently a few times. Roll out the dough into about a 10×12 inch rectangle and cut it into ¾ inch wide strips. Weave the strips over the filling and turn them under at the ends to fit the dish. Sprinkle with the remaining sugar. Bake in a preheated 375° oven for 40 minutes or until the pastry is browned and the juices bubble up. Serves eight to ten.

Last week we picked sour cherries in Door County, Wisconsin, just before returning home from vacation. After pitting and freezing most of them, I had neither the time nor the energy to make a pie, but I did make a cherry kuchen. Kuchen is the German word for cake. This recipe is quite typical of the type of pastry a German housewife would produce in her own kitchen. Fancier pastries are almost always bought at a bakery.

Since the rich crust is patted into the pan, a fruit kuchen is quick and easy to make. It has the added advantage of making very little mess during preparation. It is easier to serve if made in a springform pan, but any nine or ten inch round pan can be used.

Almost any prepared fresh fruit or dry packed frozen fruit would be satisfactory for this recipe. The amounts of fruit and sugar and the type of thickening agent are easy to vary to suit individual tastes. Remember that one and one half teaspoons of cornstarch has the same thickening power as one tablespoon of all-purpose flour.

Fruit Kuchen

Crust:
1 ½ cups flour
3 tablespoons sugar
Pinch of salt
¾ cup margarine
1 ½ tablespoons vinegar
⅛ teaspoon cinnamon (optional)

Filling:
3 to 4 cups fresh fruit
Approximately 1 ⅓ cups sugar
3 tablespoons flour

Crust: Mix the flour, sugar and salt together. Work in the margarine with a pastry blender or a fork. Mix in the vinegar. Reserve a generous half cup of the crumbs for topping. Pat the remainder into a 9 or 10 inch springform pan, covering the bottom and 1 inch up the sides of the pan.

Filling: Mix the fruit (blueberries, peaches, cherries, nectarines or plums), sugar to suit your taste, and flour. Turn this mixture into the prepared pan.

Topping: Add cinnamon to the reserved crumbs and sprinkle them over the kuchen. Bake in a preheated 400° oven for one hour. Makes eight servings.

Celebrations & Festivals

Winter Sky - Northfield   P. Lampe

Heart-shaped cookies make a special Valentine treat. You can make them in any size you like. If you don't have a cookie cutter in the size you want, make a cardboard pattern and trace around it with the point of a knife.

If you are making very large hearts, roll the dough out right on the cookie sheet, trace around the pattern and then remove the excess dough. You may want to roll the dough for very large cookies a little thicker than you normally do, so they will be less likely to break when you remove them from the cookie sheet.

The simplest way to decorate Valentine cookies is to sprinkle them with red sugar before you bake them. Or you can frost them after they are cool and inscribe them with whatever sentiments you wish. The cookies will look like giant candy hearts.

The recipe I will share with you produces a fairly firm cookie which isn't too sweet. The dough is easy to handle. You can use almost any favorite frosting recipe. Tint most of it pink, but don't forget to leave some white for the lettering. If you don't have cake decorating equipment, the pressurized cans of icing available at the food market work fine.

My icing recipe produces a frosting similar to that which bakeries use.

Sour Cream Sugar Cookies

2 cups sugar
1 cup shortening
2 eggs
1 cup sour cream
1 teaspoon vanilla
6 cups flour
1 teaspoon baking soda
½ teaspoon salt

Cream the sugar and the shortening together. Add the eggs, sour cream and vanilla; mix well. Sift or stir the flour, baking soda and salt together and add to the creamed mixture. Chill the dough in the refrigerator for at least 45 minutes. On a floured surface, roll the dough approximately one-eighth inch thick and cut it with a cookie cutter. Bake on a greased cookie sheet in a 375° oven for 8–10 minutes or until golden brown. Makes three to six dozen cookies, depending on their size.

Creamy Decorating Icing

1 cup vegetable shortening
1 teaspoon vanilla
Pinch of salt
1 pound (about 4 cups) confectioner's sugar
3 tablespoons milk

Cream the shortening with an electric mixer. Add vanilla and salt. Beat in the sugar; one cup at a time, blending well after each addition and frequently scraping the sides and bottom of the bowl with a rubber spatula to insure thorough mixing. Add the milk and beat at a high speed until light and fluffy. May be stored in the refrigerator, but rewhip before using. Makes three cups of icing.

Valentine's Day brings cards covered with hearts and cute sayings, flowers for your nearest and dearest, or sweets for your sweetie or even your friends. My daughter Sara has already told me to make sure that the makings for fudge are on the shelf, as she wants to give all her friends squares of fudge topped with candy hearts as Valentines.

At Christmas time we worked at perfecting our fudge recipe, with gifts to teachers, friends, brothers and Grandma. She even sold fudge to friends' parents who didn't have the time or inclination to make their own, yet wanted to give a homemade present.

The recipe we finally came up with contains a bit of cornstarch, which seems to insure really smooth and creamy fudge, as well as a couple of ounces of baking chocolate for a real chocolatey taste. Be sure to use real chocolate chips.

Sara's Fudge

4 cups sugar
1 tablespoon cornstarch
½ teaspoon salt
13 ounce can evaporated milk
½ cup margarine (one stick)
12 ounce package real chocolate chips
2 ounces bitter chocolate
7 ounce jar marshmallow cream

In a large, heavy saucepan, thoroughly mix together the sugar, cornstarch and salt. Add the milk and margarine and bring the mixture, stirring constantly, to a full boil which can't be stirred down over a medium high heat. Lower heat to medium and continue cooking for five minutes, stirring constantly to prevent scorching. Remove from heat and stir in the chips and chocolate, and then the marshmallow cream. Allow the mixture to cool for a few minutes and then beat it with a spoon until the mixture begins to thicken. Spread in a very well-greased 10×15 inch jelly roll pan. Cut into squares when cool. This recipe makes almost 5 pounds of fudge.

When sending fudge off in the mail, I put the warm fudge in a clean half gallon milk carton. When the fudge is cool, I fold the top of the carton down over the fudge and wrap the carton in plastic wrap, before wrapping the whole thing in brown paper and mailing off a popular package.

Beans literally fueled the expansion of our country from coast to coast. Whether you picture a Puritan family sitting at their table with heads bowed or a lone prospector hunched over his camp fire, chances are they were going to have beans for supper. Dried beans were easy to store and to transport. They were also satisfying to eat and if they produced a little gas, so be it.

We now know that our ancestors chose well when they made beans a staple of their diets. Nutritionists have shown that beans are high in protein and when combined with another grain, such as rice or wheat, provide all of the necessary amino acids. Various types of beans are a mainstay of vegetarian diets.

For many of us, old-fashioned baked beans remain a favorite. In fact, some feel that no picnic would be complete without them. We recently spent a week-end at a friend's lakeside cabin where a pot of slow-baked beans was produced to go with the brats and hot dogs. There was surprise that the recipe called for no tomatoes. These were traditional Boston baked beans, sweetened with molasses and brown sugar and seasoned with a little mustard and onion, then baked until tender. Sometimes a bit of salt pork is added, although these were delicious without it.

When I got home, I looked through my cookbooks and files for a recipe for beans with a tomato sauce. I finally found one in a vegetarian cookbook that I thought might provide the basis for experimenting.

I also found out more about beans than I really wanted to know. One author recommended adding half a teaspoon of baking soda to the water in which the beans are precooked because it helps to soften the skins so that the beans cook quicker. Another warned against using baking soda because it has an adverse affect on the flavor of the beans. Some recommended cooking the beans in the water they soaked in, while others said to change the water.

Many pointed out that the flatulence which beans sometimes produce is caused by the complex sugars that are not broken down in cooking and then are acted upon by bacteria in the intestines. If you are willing to sacrifice some nutrition, you should discard the water in which the beans are soaked, as described below. This procedure gets rid of most of the complex sugars and can avoid problems with flatulence.

I used navy beans for this tomato-sauced bean recipe although pea beans or great northerns would also be good.

Fourth of July Baked Beans

1 pound dried beans
Water
1 can tomato paste (6 ounces)
½ cup molasses
¼ cup brown sugar
2 teaspoons Dijon mustard
Pinch of red pepper
3 tablespoons soy sauce
1 tablespoon vegetable oil
1 large onion, sliced into rings

You can cook the beans according to directions on the package or follow this procedure: Soak, wash and pick over the beans, discarding any broken or darkly colored ones. Cover the beans with water and soak over night. Drain the beans and cover them with fresh water. Bring to a boil over high heat and skim off any foam that forms. Turn the heat down and cover the pan. Cook the beans for 10 minutes, drain them once more and again add fresh water to finish cooking them. Cook the covered beans until they are as soft as you want them. The baking process will not change their texture.

Combine the cooked beans, tomato paste, molasses, brown sugar, mustard, red pepper and soy sauce. If the mixture is too dry, add water until it is the consistency you desire. Place the beans in a 9×9 inch pan and cover with aluminum foil. Bake for 30 minutes in a preheated 350° oven. Meanwhile fry the onion in the oil, separating the rings, until they are a golden brown. Remove the beans from the oven and top with the onion rings. Bake, uncovered, for an additional 10 minutes. Serves six generously.

WE TEND TO THINK of Thanksgiving as a distinctively American holiday, but the custom of setting aside a day of thanks during the harvest season was centuries old by the time Plymouth Colony sat down to its famous dinner. For the Pilgrims it was a religious occasion, a time to reflect on God's blessings. The Massachusetts Bay Colony and Connecticut continued to hold an annual day of thanks in the 17th and 18th centuries and then sporadically after the American Revolution. Thanksgiving, as we know it, is a fairly modern holiday. It was not until 1859 when thirty states gave thanks on the same day.

The real credit for the holiday belongs to Mrs. Sarah J. Hale who began a campaign for a thanksgiving day in 1827 by writing editorials and petitioning governors and presidents. In 1863 she wrote, "Wise lawgivers and great patriots have acknowledged the salutary effect of appointed times for national reunions which combine religious sentiment with domestic and social enjoyment." One month later, in the midst of the Civil War, President Lincoln issued the first Thanksgiving Day Proclamation.

We may no longer be able to gather the whole family together for a feast at grandmother's house, but we can share the day with family and friends. One of our family traditions at Thanksgiving is my recipe for an Alsatian stuffing for the turkey. It may seem like a lot of work to make when you can so easily buy bread for dressing, but the main ingredient can be made ahead and frozen or just stored in a plastic bag for two or three days. So it isn't any more work on Thanksgiving Day than the simplest dressing. I'm sure you will find it worth the effort.

If a whole turkey is too big for you, have a frozen turkey sawed in half. Then you can bake the dressing in a bowl alongside the turkey for about an hour.

Alsatian Dressing

2 ½ cups flour
1 teaspoon baking soda
1 teaspoon salt
2 ½ teaspoons cream of tartar
12 ounce carton sour cream
3 eggs
1 pound pork sausage, cooked
1 teaspoon sage (optional)
Broth

Sift or stir together the flour, salt, soda and cream of tartar. Add the sour cream and stir to make a soft dough. Pat the dough lightly into a loaf and bake it in a 375° oven for 50 minutes or until it is brown and crisp. Cool. (At this point the loaf may be frozen or stored in a plastic bag.)

Crumb the loaf into a large bowl and add the sage, eggs and sausage. Moisten the mixture with broth made from giblets or diluted canned chicken broth. Mix well. Add salt and pepper to taste. Lightly stuff the turkey. Bake following the instructions that come with the bird. Extra stuffing can be baked in a dish.

Thanksgiving Dinner

Dear David,

We enjoyed talking to you last night. Your plans for cooking a Thanksgiving dinner in your college dorm kitchen sound ambitious. I fondly remember the first Thanksgiving dinner I helped make when your Dad and I were graduate students. We had a good time even if everything didn't turn out perfectly.

The Turkey:

These memories remind me to urge you to start out cautiously. Feasts have a way of growing beyond the amount of food that can reasonably be consumed. In other words, don't buy too big a turkey. A 10–12 pound bird should serve 10–12 people. The best way for you to defrost the bird will be to buy it Wednesday morning and leave it in a double brown bag until Thursday morning. It should just about be thawed out. If it's not, run cold water into the body cavity until it is. Remember to remove the neck and giblets (liver, heart, and gizzard). Sometimes they are hidden up in front under the neck skin; cook them in about two cups of water and use the resulting broth for your gravy.

Making your Dressing and Cooking the Turkey:

I'll give you a start by including the bread in the package I'm mailing today. The instructions for Alsatian dressing were in last week's News. You will have to buy the sausage, eggs, and chicken broth. If the package doesn't arrive in time, you had better buy a stuffing mix and follow the instructions on the package.

Rinse out the turkey's cavities and put the stuffing in. Don't pack it in too firmly or your bird may burst its skin before it is done. Fill the body first, and then put what is left in the neck hole and fasten the skin in place with a couple of tooth picks. Sprinkle the turkey with salt and pepper and pop it in the oven. Cook it for 20–25 minutes per pound in a 350° oven; about 3 ½ hours should do it. After a half hour, there should be enough juice in the pan to spoon over the bird. Repeat this process every half hour.

The Trimmings:

That takes care of the main part of your meal, but I do think it would be nice if you would serve something else. You could make a simple salad by placing orange slices in a circle on a small plate and putting a thin slice of cranberry jelly in the middle. If you are feeling elegant, put a lettuce leaf under the oranges. And you had better have a veggie too. Look in the frozen food section; you might even find broccoli with hollandaise or cheese sauce. You can also buy rolls. If you have an extra pan, you might want to cook some potatoes and mash them (that will take about 30 minutes).

Now for the Gravy:

Remove your turkey from the pan. Don't worry if the gravy seems to be taking awhile to make, because the turkey will carve better after it has sat for 15–20 minutes. If there is a lot of fat in the pan, take some out. Then add about six tablespoons of flour to the drippings, as well as the broth you have made from the neck and giblets and two cups of milk. Put the pan on top of the stove and bring to a boil, stirring all the while. If you are using a foil roaster, be gentle when you scrape the brown bits from the bottom of the pan.

We will miss not having you at our table, but I'm sure you will have a good time sharing the day with people you like. Bon appetit!

Love,

Mom

When my daughter was confirmed two weeks ago, she wanted our family's traditional celebratory dinner, roast beef and Yorkshire pudding. Yorkshire pudding is wonderful stuff. It is the ultimate accompaniment to roast beef.

Since Yorkshire pudding is a great favorite at our house, I have done quite a bit of experimenting with the basic recipe. I have found that the best pudding, the one that rises the highest and obtains a lovely crisp crust, is made using either skim milk or one cup of whole milk and one cup of water. Also, letting the batter sit in the refrigerator for several hours before baking makes for a more tender pudding. This allows any air that was beaten into the dough to escape and the gluten in the flour to relax.

The baking pan should be sizzling hot before you add the batter. This insures that the pudding won't stick to the pan and will have a crisp bottom. The initial very hot oven makes the pudding puff up, and the lower final temperature insures that it bakes through without becoming too brown.

The English once served Yorkshire pudding in a separate course before the meat, knowing that it was difficult to resist. Diners would eat lots of pudding and therefore desire less meat. Nowadays, they are usually served together. Since the roasts I cook seem to have very little fat, which is called for in the pudding recipe, I use oil in baking the pudding and save the meat drippings for gravy.

The recipe can easily be cut in half for a smaller family and baked in a square 8 or 9 inch pan.

Yorkshire Pudding

2 cups flour
1 teaspoon salt
2 cups skim milk (or 1 cup whole milk and 1 cup water)
4 eggs
¼ cup oil or meat drippings

Stir together the flour and salt. Add the milk and beat vigorously until smooth. Add the eggs one at a time, beating well after each addition. The batter should be the consistency of heavy cream. Refrigerate the batter for at least two hours.

Pour the oil into a 9×13 pan and place it in the oven to heat while warming the oven to 450°. Add the batter to the hot pan and bake for 15 minutes. Reduce the oven temperature to 350° and bake for an additional 15 minutes. Serve immediately. Serves four to six.

The American Heritage Dictionary defines neighbor as "one who lives near or next to another." If one is lucky, that neighbor may turn into a friend: "a person whom one knows, likes and trusts." The dictionary definition doesn't include sharing, but I think that is also an important component of friendship whether the sharing is of a dream, a sorrow, a family celebration, a solution for political problems, or something simpler such as the use of a tool, a cup of coffee, a recipe.

I fondly remember an afternoon I spent in the kitchen of the Moravian Church parsonage, learning to make Moravian Sugar Cake. I have made this recipe many times since then. It has become a family favorite. I've served it to guests and even given it as a Christmas present. Every time I make it, I think of my friend, even though she is no longer a neighbor.

The original recipe calls for baking the cake in three 9×2 round pans, but I usually bake it in two jelly-roll pans, 11×16, which makes a slightly thinner cake. This cake freezes very well. I freeze it in portions just big enough for us each to have a piece for Sunday morning breakfast.

Moravian Sugar Cake

Cake:
2 cups milk
1 package active dry yeast
½ cup warm water (110°)
1 cup cooled mashed potatoes
½ teaspoon salt
8 ½ cups flour
½ cup shortening
½ cup butter
2 eggs
1 cup sugar

Filling:
1 cup firmly-packed brown sugar
½ cup melted butter

Topping:
1 cup firmly-packed brown sugar
1 teaspoon cinnamon

Scald the milk and cool it. Dissolve the yeast in the warm water and let it sit until foamy. In a large bowl, combine the milk, yeast, potatoes, and salt. (If you don't have any leftover mashed potatoes, instant mashed potatoes will do.) Mix well. Add four cups of the flour, beating to combine it thoroughly. Cover the bowl with plastic wrap or a damp towel and let the dough rise until light; this will take about one hour, depending on the temperature of your kitchen.

Add the butter, shortening, eggs and sugar, beating well. Then add the remaining flour gradually, about a cup at a time, mixing well after each addition. Spread the dough in greased pans (three deep, 9 inch round pans or two jelly-roll pans).

Let the dough rise, covered with a damp towel until it is doubled, about one hour. With a floured finger make an indentation about every inch in the dough. Mix together 1 cup of brown sugar and the melted butter and put a tiny bit in each indentation. Sprinkle the remaining brown sugar, mixed with the cinnamon, over the tops of the cakes.

Bake in a preheated 375° oven for 12 to 15 minutes, watching carefully so that the sugar doesn't get too brown.

I DON'T KNOW WHY, but people who stay out of the kitchen as much as possible during most of the year are drawn to it as the Christmas season approaches. There is something about doing the Christmas baking which is almost a religious experience for some people. Perhaps it is the miracle of the transformation of everyday butter, sugar, flour and eggs into something very special, something which is so different in smell, taste and appearance.

Or perhaps memory plays the most important part in drawing us to the kitchen at Christmas time. We want to recreate the tastes and smells that we associate with the holiday season and share with our children this piece of cultural heritage, so that someday their children too will know that their roots came from Scandinavia, Germany, England or wherever. There may be no one left to tell how Christmas was celebrated in the old country, but the krumkake or springerli will be there as a reminder that we didn't always just eat chocolate-chip cookies.

Generosity may also call us to the kitchen. It is the time of year to share good things with family and friends, whether we do it by delivering a basket of fresh baked goodies to a neighbor or opening up our homes to family and friends. Good things seem even better when shared.

Here is a recipe for a drop cookie, chock full of cranberries and nuts, which makes a pleasant addition to any cookie tray. It is a soft not too sweet cookie which is quite pretty with its red flecks of cranberries. The cookie sheets must be well greased or you will have trouble removing the cookies from the pan. They must also be removed from the pan while they are hot. I was once interrupted by the telephone just as I had taken a pan of these cookies from the oven; by the time I had finished talking, the cookies were pretty well welded to the pan. I just put the pan back in the oven for a minute to slightly soften the cookies, and then they came off without any trouble.

Orange Cranberry Nut Cookies

½ cup butter or margarine
1 cup white sugar
¾ cup brown sugar, packed
¼ cup milk
2 tablespoons orange juice
1 teaspoon grated orange rind (optional)
1 egg
3 cups flour
1 teaspoon baking powder
¼ teaspoon baking soda
½ teaspoon salt
1 cup chopped nuts
2 ½ cups coarsely chopped cranberries

Cream the butter and both sugars together. Beat in the milk, orange juice, orange rind and egg. Combine the flour, baking powder, baking soda and salt. Add this to the creamed mixture, mixing well. Stir in the nuts and cranberries.

Drop the batter by teaspoonfuls onto well-greased cookie sheets and bake in a preheated 375° oven for 10–15 minutes, until slightly browned. Remove the cookies from the pans immediately and cool on racks before storing. Makes 8 to 10 dozen small cookies.

I GUESS IT'S ABOUT time to decide what will be served for Christmas dinner. In many cases I know that this doesn't take a lot of planning because the meal is pretty well set by family tradition, be the main course turkey, ham, roast beef, or a buffet of Scandinavian specialties.

In my family, it's roast beef and Yorkshire pudding for the main course, red and green gelatin salad for Christmas color, and the usual vegetables and relishes. But for dessert, I always try to have something different. This year I am making a Finnish Christmas prune cake. One of the advantages of this recipe is that both the torte base and prune topping can be made up to three days ahead of time and easily combined on Christmas day just before serving.

I'll close this column with the wish that is on the Christmas cards my daughter chose this year: "May Christmas find you in a warm, cheery place."

Finnish Christmas Prune Cake

Cake:
¾ cup butter or margarine, softened
½ cup, minus 1 tablespoon, sugar
3 eggs
⅔ cup flour
1 teaspoon baking powder

Topping:
1 ¼ cup cooked, pitted prunes, puréed
1 teaspoon grated orange rind
Sugar to taste
½ cup heavy cream, whipped and sweetened

Cake: In a large bowl, cream the butter and sugar together until light and fluffy. Add the eggs one at a time, beating well after each addition. Sift or stir together the flour and baking powder and gradually add it to the egg mixture, stirring gently to form a stiff batter.

Spread the batter in a well-greased and floured 9 inch square pan and bake in a preheated 350° oven for 20–25 minutes or until a toothpick inserted in middle of the cake comes out clean. Cool the cake on a rack for about 10 minutes and then remove it from the pan. When thoroughly cooled, the cake may be well wrapped and refrigerated until serving time (up to three days).

Topping: Blend the prune purée with the orange peel and add sugar to taste; if the purée is too thin, thicken it by slowly cooking over very low heat while stirring frequently. Spread the purée on top of the cake and decorate with whipped cream piped around the edges; or simply garnish each serving with whipped cream. Serves nine.

Have you ever wondered just what a sugar plum actually is? "The Night Before Christmas" has made the term sugar plum synonymous with Christmas goodies. In fact, *The American Heritage Dictionary* defines sugar plum as a small piece of sugary candy.

A real sugar plum is a green gage plum which has been dried, pitted, rolled in granulated sugar and then heated until the sugar is glazed. Sugar plums are then cooled and stored in a tightly lidded container. This confection is a specialty of a convent in Portugal where the nuns make them for export. The dry, sunny climate helps to grow a superior plum and later to dry the fruit properly without having it shrivel.

Sugar was not in common use until well into the seventeenth century. Before that time honey was used as a sweetener. No one knows exactly when sugar was first made although it probably was first manufactured in India from sugar cane; it was first described as Indian salt. By the late fifteenth century, the process for crystallizing sugar had been devised.

Sugar was sold only in apothecaries and was one of the most expensive of foodstuffs. Despite its price, one of its earliest uses was to candy fruits. At one time a sugar plum must truly have represented the finest treat possible.

Christmas Joy

Happy hearts
Lots of love
Memories, happy and sad
Hope, faith and self control
Patience
Understanding
Traditions
Smiles
Song
Sugar plums

Combine hearts and love. Carefully fold in memories and hopes. Let stand while you think about what Christmas really means. Now add faith and a measure of self control. Blend together patience and understanding and add to the first mixture. Season to taste with traditions. Allow to grow until double. Frost with smiles, sprinkle with a song and garnish with dreams of sugar plums. Share with friends and family. Yield: one Merry Christmas.

Cookies & Bars

Victorian Queens   P Lampe   1972

BAKELSER, SMABROD, KEKS, KOEKJES, tortas, biscuits, cookies. Whatever they are called, they are favorite treats. The almost universal appeal of cookies is somewhat surprising as it was not very common to make cookies at home before the 1890s, when kitchen ranges came into common use. Before that time, baking had to be done in ovens set into the side of fireplaces or on griddles set over hot coals. Since one of the factors which affects the success of cookie baking is a constant oven temperature, it's easy to see why few cooks made the effort.

With modern mixers and ovens, cookie baking is relatively easy. A pan of cookies should bake in about 9–12 minutes in a 375° oven. Leave your kitchen exhaust fan off, and your nose will tell you when they are done. You can set up a production line if you have three cookie sheets. Remember cookies should be baked on a sheet or very shallow pan.

Prepare one pan of cookies and place it on the bottom rack of your oven. Then prepare another pan. Place the first pan on the top shelf to finish baking while putting the second pan on the bottom shelf. Rotating the pans helps the cookies to bake evenly. Now prepare the third pan so you are all ready to put it on the bottom rack when you remove the cookies that are done. It is amazing how many cookies you can bake in a short time using this method.

Now after telling you how to bake cookies, I'll give you a recipe for an unbaked cookie which adds pleasant variety to a cookie plate. When my children were younger, they did not like either nuts or coconut but by chance they loved these balls which they called "mud balls," a very descriptive name.

Chocolate Coconut Balls

½ cup milk
2 egg yolks, slightly beaten
½ cup sugar
⅓ cup flour
⅛ teaspoon salt
2 tablespoons butter
1 teaspoon vanilla
1 cup real chocolate chips
½ cup chopped nuts
1 four ounce can of coconut

Mix the milk and egg yolks in the top pan of a double boiler. Sift or stir together the flour, sugar and salt, and add it to the milk mixture. Add the butter. Cook over boiling water, stirring constantly, until very thick. Remove from heat and add the vanilla and chocolate chips. Stir until the chocolate melts and is thoroughly blended in. Stir in the nuts. Chill in the refrigerator. Form into small balls and roll in coconut. Store in the refrigerator.

There is an exhibition of contemporary shopping bags—titled "The Brown Bag Has Gone"—currently on display at Carleton College. If you are looking at the spring beauty of the Carleton campus, you might want to stop and witness the transformations the humble brown bag has undergone since it was invented by Charles Stillwell in 1883 and made of brown kraft paper.

The shopping bag has gone from being a strictly utilitarian object to being a status symbol or work of art. Bags have become a major source of free advertising both for the companies that provide them and the people who carry them. The bag you choose to carry can make a statement about where you have been, whether to the Tower of London or the local supermarket; what you are interested in, art, architecture, sports, or food; and the image you desire to project, whether flamboyant or conservative.

Most of the bags in the Carleton display are plastic, as are over thirty percent of all shopping bags. The size ranges from one designed to hold a single chocolate truffle to a king-sized one large enough to hold all the bargains from an annual white sale. Some bags give factual information while others make an artistic statement.

Bags don't taste good, but you could bake something that does, put it in a bag and have a picnic.

Rhubarb Bars

3 eggs
2 ½ cups sugar
1 teaspoon vanilla
6 tablespoons (⅜ cup) water
10 tablespoons butter or margarine, melted and cooled
2 ¼ cups flour
3 cups thinly-sliced rhubarb
½ cup chopped nuts or raisins

Beat the eggs and gradually add the sugar. Add the vanilla and water and mix well. Add the melted butter and mix again. Add the flour and beat for three minutes at the medium speed of an electric mixer. Fold in the rhubarb and nuts and pour the batter into a well-greased and floured 9×13 inch cake pan.

Bake in a preheated 375° oven for about 40 minutes. When they are done, the tops of the bars will be lightly browned and they will have begun to pull away from the sides of the pan. Makes 18–24 bars.

School starts next week and with it, for some of us, the seemingly endless succession of brown bags to be filled with lunches you hope are nourishing and something your children will eat and not just discard. My daughter suggested sharing with you a recipe for peanut butter bars. They require no baking and are quick and easy to make. In fact, the kids can make them. A warning note should be added: some people find these irresistible and have been known to eat a whole recipe, or it least most of one, at one sitting.

Peanut Butter Bars

1 cup butter or margarine
1 cup peanut butter
2 ½ cups powdered sugar
2 cups graham cracker crumbs (35–40 graham crackers)
6 to 12 ounces semi-sweet or milk chocolate chips

Melt the butter and peanut butter together in a large pan. Stir in the sugar and graham cracker crumbs. Pat into a buttered 9×13 pan. Melt the chocolate chips and spread over the top. Cool and cut into squares.

HAPPY BIRTHDAY TO YOU. Happy birthday to you. Happy birthday dear chocolate cookie. Happy birthday to you. Yes, one of America's great contributions to the culinary world is fifty years old.

Back in the fall of 1930, Ruth Wakefield chopped up a semi-sweet chocolate bar and added it to the cookie dough she was making in the kitchen of the Toll House Inn near Whitman, Mass. The result is history.

Her cookie recipe became so popular that Nestle soon made a bar of chocolate that was scored so that it could easily be broken into small pieces. Then in 1939, a machine capable of producing little pieces of chocolate was developed, and the chocolate chip as we know it was born.

I use my mother's recipe, which originally called for six ounces of chopped chocolate. I think it makes one of the best cookies around. A few years ago my mother faced a domestic crisis. One of her granddaughters had cleaned out her recipe box. All of the old, grease spotted recipe cards were thrown away. That is not the way to straighten out your recipes. Luckily I had a copy of the old favorite and mother was soon back in production.

There is quite a bit of discussion in our house whether or not the cookies should even be baked. More than once, cookie dough has been the choice as the special birthday treat. Even though a bowl of dough adorned with candles looks pretty silly, it does taste good.

When family members are going camping, I make a camping cookie by adding half a cup of wheat germ and ¾ cup of ground nuts to the dough. I then bake cookies that are about seven inches in diameter. After wrapping them individually, I bag them one per person per day and they form the backbone of trail lunches.

So celebrate and bake a batch or two or three....

Chocolate Crunch Cookies

1 cup shortening
¾ cup granulated sugar
¾ cup brown sugar
2 eggs
2 ½ cups flour
1 teaspoon salt
1 teaspoon soda
1 teaspoon hot water
1 teaspoon vanilla
1 cup nuts – optional
1 six ounce package chocolate chips

Cream the shortening and sugars together well. Add the eggs and beat thoroughly. Sift or stir the flour and salt. Add this to the first mixture alternately with soda, which has been dissolved in the hot water. Add the vanilla. Stir in the nuts and chocolate chips. Drop by rounded spoonfuls on greased cookie sheets and bake in a 375° oven.

Once again it is time to face the question of what to put in that brown bag that goes off to school each day. I know well the quirks in taste that can develop, having had a son who carried his lunch every day for twelve years and never took a sandwich. It was quite a shock to have lunch with him in a college dining room and watch him wolf down a sandwich with the comment, "Oh, I eat all sorts of junk now." Education can be broadening in more than one way.

My daughter suggested a good lunchtime treat recipe, which is called 99 Cookies. I usually get about 60 cookies and my mother claims to have made 111 out of one batch. But no matter how many cookies you get, I think you will like them. They are a rather sweet, very crisp cookie with that nice light texture, which is characteristic of cookies containing cream of tartar. If you don't like nuts, try substituting sunflower seeds or use a little more oatmeal or Rice Krispies.

99 Cookies

1 cup brown sugar
1 cup white sugar
1 cup margarine
1 cup oil
1 egg
1 ½ teaspoons vanilla
3 ½ cups flour
¼ teaspoon salt
1 teaspoon soda
1 teaspoon cream of tartar
1 cup oatmeal
1 cup Rice Krispies
1 cup coconut
½ cup nuts

Beat together the sugars, margarine, oil, egg, and vanilla until light and creamy. Sift or stir the flour, salt, soda, and cream of tartar together and stir into the shortening mixture. Fold in the remaining ingredients. Drop by rounded teaspoonful on ungreased cookie sheets and bake in a preheated 350° oven until nicely browned, approximately 15 minutes.

"WOULD YOU BE WILLING to bring a pan of bars?"

How I hate to hear that request echoing over the phone. I really don't know why, but I classify bars as things I would rather not bother with in the kitchen. In my opinion, the perfect recipe for a bar should be extremely easy to make and contain only ingredients that one has on hand; one should make enough to share and have some left over for home consumption.

This first recipe comes close to fulfilling these conditions. Although it calls for a cup of sliced almonds, something I usually do not have on hand, you can sprinkle on a few more miniature marshmallows and no one will miss them.

Have you ever wondered where marshmallows got their name? Originally this soft white confection was made with sugar and the root of a plant called the marsh mallow, which was a native of Europe and was naturalized into the marshes of our East Coast. The sticky sap from the root was used to soothe sore throats. Today, marshmallows are made of sugar or corn syrup, gelatin, egg whites and various stabilizers.

Caramel Heavenlies

12 double graham crackers
2 cups miniature marshmallows
¾ cup butter or margarine
¾ cup brown sugar
1 teaspoon cinnamon
1 teaspoon vanilla
1 cup sliced almonds
1 cup flaked coconut

Line a buttered jelly-roll pan (10¼ x 15½) with a single layer of graham crackers. You may need a few extra pieces to fill in the edges. Sprinkle the marshmallows over the graham crackers. In a small saucepan cook together the butter and brown sugar until the sugar dissolves. Add the cinnamon and vanilla to this mixture and then drizzle it over the top of the marshmallow layer. Sprinkle the almonds

and coconut on top and bake in a preheated 350° oven for 10 to 12 minutes. Cool in the pan, then cut into squares (approximately three inches to a side) and cut each square in half to make two triangles. Makes 30 good-sized pieces.

This next recipe is really a thin cheesecake and is almost too elegant to be called a bar.

Cheesecake Squares

Crust and topping:
⅓ cup brown sugar
5 tablespoons butter or margarine
1 cup flour
¼ cup chopped walnuts

Filling:
½ cup granulated sugar
1 eight ounce package cream cheese
1 egg
2 tablespoons milk
1 tablespoon lemon juice
½ teaspoon vanilla

Cream together the butter and brown sugar. Add the flour and walnuts, mixing well. Set aside a cup of this mixture for the topping and press the remainder into the bottom of an 8 inch square pan. Bake in a preheated 350° oven for 10–12 minutes.

Meanwhile, blend together the cream cheese and granulated sugar until the mixture is smooth. Add the egg, milk, lemon juice and vanilla. Beat well. Spread this mixture over the baked crust, sprinkle it with the reserved crumbs, return it to the oven, and bake for an additional 25 minutes. Cool and then chill until serving time. Makes 16 two inch squares.

CHOCOLATE IS A GIFT from the Aztecs. Montezuma shared his favorite cocoa-like drink with Cortez. The words chocolate and cocoa come from the Aztec word cacahuatl. Today the cacao tree is cultivated in Africa and Southeast Asia, as well as tropical America, and chocolate has become a world-wide favorite flavor. Almost everyone has a favorite chocolate treat.

Chocolate Syrup Brownies

1 cup sugar
½ cup margarine
4 eggs
16 ounce can chocolate syrup
1 cup flour
½ cup chopped nuts (optional)

Cream together the sugar and margarine. Add the eggs and beat well. Stir in the chocolate syrup and then fold in the flour and nuts. Bake in a well-greased 9×13 pan in a preheated 350° oven for 25–30 minutes. Do not overbake. When cooled, the brownies may be dusted with powdered sugar or frosted.

If you are looking for a real chocolate fix, you could frost the brownies with my favorite fudge frosting. If your conscience is bothering you, you can easily cut this recipe in half and still have enough frosting to cover the top of a 9×13 pan of brownies.

Fudge Frosting

6 tablespoons butter or margarine
6 tablespoons milk
1 ½ cups sugar
½ cup chocolate chips

Combine the butter, milk and sugar in a large sauce pan. Cook, stirring constantly, until the mixture comes to a full boil. Boil for 30 seconds. Remove from the heat and stir in the chocolate chips. Continue stirring until the frosting begins to thicken. Spread as desired.

GHIRARDELLI SQUARE IN SAN FRANCISCO is a maze of old factory buildings, which have been converted into a beehive of shops and restaurants. Tucked into one corner of this conglomerate is the Ghirardelli Chocolate Manufactory, Soda Fountain & Candy Shop (founded in the 1850s).

There one can indulge in many exotic chocolate treats while smelling cocoa beans being roasted, watching chocolate liquor drip from the mills and seeing huge vats of chocolate being kneaded. It's enough to send your sweet tooth into a state of shock, even if chocolate isn't your very favorite flavor.

Here is the recipe for Cable Car Chocolate Brownies, which appeared in the 1980s on the box of Ghirardelli cocoa. It makes one of the best brownies I have ever tasted.

Cable Car Chocolate Brownies

2 eggs
¾ cup sugar
1 teaspoon vanilla
½ cup melted butter or margarine
¾ cup cocoa
⅔ cup flour
¼ teaspoon baking powder
¼ teaspoon salt
½ cup chopped walnuts (optional)

Using a spoon, stir the eggs with the sugar and vanilla and then add the butter. Sift or stir the cocoa with the flour, baking powder and salt. Stir this into the egg mixture; add the nuts. Spread into a well-greased 8 or 9 inch square pan. Bake in a preheated 350° oven for 20–30 minutes, depending on whether you like chewy or cake-like brownies. Cool and cut into squares.

Granola bars have become a popular American snack. They are nutritious and taste good. They make a good after school treat and are handy to carry in a pocket while hiking. Unfortunately, they are also fairly expensive. However, you can make them for much less than they cost to buy.

A friend recently sent me a granola-bar recipe that she had made in school. It is simply a mixture of peanut butter, honey, dried skim milk and granola—tasty and very nutritious.

It is also the beginning point for making a snack which includes your own favorites. Try adding raisins or other chopped, dried fruits, nuts or seeds, or even mini-chocolate chips for a custom-made snack. You can easily add ½ to 1 cup of additional solids to this recipe.

Karla's Granola Bars

1 cup peanut butter
1 cup honey
1 cup instant, dried skim milk
1 cup granola

Mix the honey and peanut butter together until well blended; this is easier to accomplish if you do it in a large sauce pan over very low heat. Stir in the dried milk until thoroughly mixed. Stir in the granola; add any additional goodies you desire. Press into a well-buttered 9×13 cake pan and chill. Cut into the desired size bars and wrap each one in plastic wrap; if the bars seem a little sticky, roll in additional granola. Makes approximately 24 bars.

Even the National Geographic magazine has gotten on the bandwagon, with a 24-page cover story on the origins and production of chocolate. In the 18th century the great botanist Linnaeus named the South American tree, which bears the pods that can be turned into chocolate. He chose the name Theobroma cacao or food of the gods. Over the past two centuries many people have come to agree with Linnaeus' evaluation of chocolate. All cacao is cultivated within twenty degrees of the equator, but it is eaten all over the world. The Norwegians and English are the champion consumers, eating over sixteen pounds per capita in 1982.

Chocolate has always been something of a status symbol. The ancient Aztecs used the seed pods as currency; wily Spaniards established cacao plantations as money farms. Today there are people willing to pay over $50 a pound for fine handmade chocolates. Chocolate seems to engender a feeling of well-being in many people. Chemists have now found that it contains minute amounts of phenylethylamine, which is also present in the human brain. This may be the reason why chocolate has become a traditional gift for a loved one or is served to special guests, but many of us eat chocolate or chocolate-flavored food just because we think it tastes good.

Here is a recipe for a soft frosted chocolate cookie which is fantastic. If you are in a real mood for chocolate, try substituting mini-chocolate chips for the nuts. Remember that buttermilk is available in half-pint cartons.

Buttermilk Chocolate Cookies

Cookies:
½ cup butter or margarine, softened
1 cup brown sugar, packed
2 eggs
2 ounces semi-sweet chocolate, melted
1 ½ cups flour
¼ teaspoon baking soda
1 teaspoon baking powder
½ cup buttermilk
½ cup chopped nuts

Frosting:
⅓ cup powdered sugar
3 teaspoons cocoa
1 ½ tablespoons butter or margarine
¼ teaspoon vanilla
Milk

Cookies: Cream together the butter and brown sugar. Add the eggs, one at a time, beating well after each addition. Add the chocolate and stir well. Sift or stir together the flour, baking soda and baking powder and add this mixture alternately with the buttermilk to the butter mixture, beating well after each addition. Stir in the nuts.

Drop the batter by teaspoonfuls onto a well-greased baking sheet. Bake in a preheated 325° oven for 10 minutes. Remove the cookies from the pan and frost them while they are still hot.

Frosting: Mix together the sugar, cocoa, butter and vanilla. Add just enough milk to make the mixture spreadable. Spread the frosting on the cookies. The recipe yields about three dozen cookies.

I STILL HAVE THREE of the lemons left that I bought more than six weeks ago in Arizona. The skins have become dried out and hard, but the fruit inside is still fresh and juicy. I plan to use them up by making a batch of lemon bars.

Here is my favorite lemon bar recipe. The crust is particularly good; it tastes almost like shortbread. I think that it is impossible to overbeat the eggs and granulated sugar in this recipe, and the fluffier the egg-sugar mixture is, the lighter the lemon layer will be.

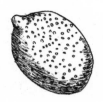

Really Lemony Bars

¾ cup butter or margarine
⅓ cup powdered sugar
1 ½ cups flour
3 eggs
1 ½ cups granulated sugar
⅓ cup lemon juice
1 teaspoon baking powder
¼ cup flour
Powdered sugar

In a medium-sized bowl, combine the butter, powdered sugar and 1½ cups flour. Using a fork, or your fingers, blend until the mixture resembles coarse crumbs. Press the crumb mixture into the bottom of a 9×13 pan and bake in a preheated 350° oven for 15–20 minutes, or until the edges begin to brown. Cool before topping with the lemon mixture.

In a large bowl, beat the eggs until they are uniform in color. Gradually add the granulated sugar and continue beating until the mixture is pale and fluffy. Stir in the lemon juice. Mix together ¼ cup flour and the baking powder and fold into the egg mixture. Spoon this topping over the crust. Bake in a 350° oven for 20–25 minutes, or until the lemon filling is firm. Cool in the pan. Sprinkle the top with powdered sugar. Cut into bars. The recipe makes about 20 generous bars.

This recipe for a simple butter cookie is for dessert lovers. The surprise is the use of almond flavoring. The cookies can be frozen in small plastic containers and do not have to be thawed before serving. I think that they would make good Christmas cookies if they were rolled in colored instead of granulated sugar, with each cookie topped with a whole blanched almond.

Almond Butter Cookies

1 cup butter or margarine
½ cup granulated sugar
1 teaspoon almond extract
2 cups flour
Additional sugar

Cream the butter. Add the sugar and beat until the mixture is light and fluffy. Add the almond extract and mix well. Stir in the flour and then chill the dough.

Roll the chilled dough into 1 inch balls, roll the balls in the additional sugar and place the cookies on an ungreased cookie sheet. Flatten the cookies with a cookie stamp or fork. Bake in a preheated 350° oven for 12–15 minutes. Remove from the pan and cool on a rack. Makes three dozen cookies.

Desserts

"Nag, Nag"   P Lampe 1978

Strawberries

IT'S STRAWBERRY TIME! I know that we can purchase strawberries most of the year, but now is the time when we can go out and pick truly ripe berries which are a deep red all the way through, those plump berries which smell and taste so good. It is always nice to find that something you like is actually good for you. Strawberries are high in Vitamin C and rich in potassium and iron and, perhaps best of all, contain only fifty-five calories per cup.

Strawberries are delicious just by themselves, but often it is possible to transform them into something really special with just a little work. For example, strawberries sweetened with a little sugar and swimming in ice-cold cream must be a heaven inspired combination, and then there is strawberries and ice cream. At least once each season I make the trek out to the Dairy Queen for a pint of soft-packed ice cream which to me seems especially good with berries.

Sweetened strawberries marinated in a little balsamic vinegar have to be eaten to be believed. Good traditional balsamic vinegar seems to have a unique way of bringing out the strawberry taste. But if you don't have any balsamic vinegar, try marinating them in some freshly-squeezed orange juice.

Then we can go on to more esoteric preparations. Chocolate dipped strawberries, which sell for about 75 cents each in gourmet shops, are really easy to make at home. Just remember that the berries must be absolutely dry or the chocolate won't stick, and use good quality semi-sweet chocolate. Leave the stems and hulls on the berries and dip about ⅔ of each one into the melted chocolate. Place on a rack over waxed paper to drain. Refrigerate if necessary to get the chocolate to harden.

Strawberries are sometimes served in a raspberry purée and called strawberries cardinal, but since the raspberry and strawberry seasons really don't overlap in Minnesota, you might want to try serving strawberries in a strawberry purée. Wash 1 quart of berries, then hull and halve them. Place one cup of the berries in a blender or food processor and add about ¼ cup lemon juice and ⅓ cup sugar. Process until the mixture is smooth. Pour the purée over the remaining berries, stir and refrigerate for about an hour before serving. Serves four. This may also be used as an ice cream or shortcake topping. Adjust the sweetness to your taste.

A fresh tasting dessert can be made by mixing together 1 cup of fresh sliced strawberries, 2 tablespoons of honey, 1 tablespoon of lemon juice and 1 cup of ricotta cheese and processing them together in a blender or food processor until smooth and light. Transfer the mixture to a pint container and freeze. Serve when firm but not quite hard. If it is frozen solid, allow it to stand at room temperature about 10 minutes before serving. Serves three or four.

Or you might make a simple strawberry soup by puréeing 2 cups of sliced berries with an 8 ounce container of strawberry yogurt until smooth. Stir in enough white wine (about ½ cup) to obtain the consistency you desire. Chill thoroughly for several hours. Serves four.

Finally, you might like to try adding a few strawberries to a tossed salad or your favorite chicken salad.

As the old banana commercial used to say, "Any way you eat them, it's impossible to beat them!"

When the first locally-grown strawberries are fresh from the field, I think that I enjoy them best with no additions. But since I tend to get carried away when picking berries and always end up with more than I had intended to pick, I serve them in a variety of ways.

The other evening I planned to make a stir fry using fresh shrimp, sugar snap peas, a little garlic and fresh oriental noodles. I wanted a dessert to go with the meal since I had not planned on either soup or salad. I decided to make an old favorite, almond float, and serve it topped with sliced strawberries. It would also be good served with sliced fresh peaches.

Almond Float

Pudding:
1 envelope unflavored gelatin
1 cup water (⅓ cup cold; ⅔ cup boiling)
⅓ cup sugar
1 cup milk
1 teaspoon almond extract

Almond sugar syrup:
⅓ cup sugar
2 cups water
½ to 1 teaspoon almond extract

Pudding: Soften the gelatin in ⅓ cup of cold water. Add ⅔ cup of boiling water and stir until the gelatin is dissolved. Then add the sugar and stir until it is dissolved. Add the milk and almond flavoring and mix well. Pour the pudding into an 8 inch square pan and chill until set. Cut into ½ inch cubes and place in serving dishes. Top with fruit and several spoonfuls of the almond sugar syrup. Serves six to eight.

Almond sugar syrup: Mix together the sugar, water, and almond extract and chill.

LOCAL STRAWBERRIES ARE RIPENING now. That means redder, riper, tastier berries are available in our own gardens, pick-your-own farms or at the farmers' market. When the berries are so good, my favorite way of serving them is to place a spoonful of powdered sugar in the center of a saucer and then place a circle of freshly washed berries around the sugar. This allows each person to use as little or as much sugar as he/she wishes.

One of the classic ways of serving almost any fresh summer fruit—strawberries, raspberries, blueberries, peaches—is with a Zabaglione or Sabayon sauce. The classic version is made with Marsala, an Italian dessert wine; it is served warm with or without fruit. The sauce may also be made with Madeira or sherry.

I will give a recipe which uses dry sherry. Also, since in the summertime a hot stove isn't a favorite place to be at the end of a meal, this version may be made ahead of time and refrigerated. It has a little more sugar than the classic version, which seems to stabilize the sauce.

Cold Zabaglione Sauce

4 pasteurized egg yolks
¾ cup sugar
¾ cup dry sherry

In the top half of a double boiler, beat the egg yolks until they are thick and lemon colored. Gradually beat in the sugar, and then add the sherry. Place the pan over, but not in, hot water and continue to beat until the sauce is very thick. The water should just simmer, not boil. This should take 8–10 minutes.

Set the double boiler top in a pan of ice water and continue beating the sauce until it is cool. Refrigerate until ready to serve.

A simple custard sauce also goes well with fresh fruit. Remember any custard must be cooked slowly to help deter curdling, which is caused by the protein in the egg being denatured by too much heat.

Custard Sauce

4 pasteurized egg yolks
¼ cup sugar
⅛ teaspoon salt
2 cups milk
1 teaspoon vanilla

In the top pan of a double boiler combine the egg yolks, sugar and salt. In another pan heat the milk just until it steams and then stir it very slowly into the yolk mixture. Cook over simmering water, stirring constantly until the mixture coats the spoon (8–10 minutes). Remove the pan from the hot water and stir in the vanilla. Cool the custard and refrigerate until ready to serve.

A LIGHT DESSERT WHICH is quite easy to produce is a bowl of chilled seedless green grapes topped with a spoonful of Devonshire cream and a sprinkling of brown sugar. The English Devonshire cream, like the French crème fraîche and the German quark, is a cultured milk product which is not commercially available locally but can be made at home.

Besides being good served with fruit, Devonshire cream also provides a cool weather treat when served with hot scones and raspberry jam. This is a traditional English tea treat and is also good for a weekend breakfast or morning coffee.

Devonshire Cream

1 package cream cheese (3 oz)
⅓ cup whipping cream

Soften the cream cheese by mashing it with a fork. Slowly add the cream, stirring until smooth. Chill before using. Serve with fresh fruit, such as grapes, topping it with a sprinkling of brown sugar, or serve it with hot scones and jam.

Scones

2 cups flour
2 teaspoons baking powder
2 teaspoons sugar
½ teaspoon salt
¼ cup butter or margarine
2 eggs
½ cup cream or milk

Sift or stir the first four ingredients together. Work in the butter with a fork. Stir the eggs and cream together in another bowl and then add to the flour mixture.

The dough should be just firm enough to handle. Turn it onto a floured surface and knead a few times. Pat it into an oblong, ¾ inch thick, and cut it into diamonds with a knife. Brush it lightly with water and sprinkle with sugar. Bake on a greased cookie sheet for 15 minutes at 450°. Makes twelve or more scones.

As I sat down to breakfast on Christmas morning, I was greeted with a chorus, "Put this in your column, Mom. People will really like it." I had made churros for a breakfast treat.

When my husband was on sabbatical leave, we spent a year in Germany and found the weather abominable. It rained every day from the middle of September through Christmas. Since it was apparent the sun was not going to come to us, we went looking for it. The day after Christmas we set off for southern Spain in our old Volkswagen camper.

Our trip proved to be one of those once in a lifetime adventures. We arrived at the height of the orange harvest and never again would we be able to eat a tangerine without thinking, "Remember the ones in Spain." We visited white-washed mountain villages and shopped in native markets. We walked through the peppermint-striped arches of the mosque at Cordoba and ate paella cooked over a fire of corn stalks on a windswept Mediterranean beach. We camped in the largest palm grove in Europe and watched the harvest of dates as we ate lunch.

We were also lucky enough to stay in several of Spain's renowned government-run inns. We stayed in one parador that was not yet finished, clinging to the rocks on the Costa del Sol and one which had been a 16th-century palace in the tiny town of Ubeda, in the midst of fields of olive and almond trees.

This brings us back to the recipe for churros. Breakfast was included with the price of a parador room. And lovely breakfasts they were, especially when compared with what I could produce on the two-burner camp stove. One of the best things was the large basket of fresh breads that arrived at the table first. The family's favorite was soon apparent—some long crispy things which were covered with sugar. We couldn't guess what they were made of and our lack of Spanish made it impossible for me to ask.

When we got home, a little research produced the recipe for Churros Madrilenos. The treat we all enjoyed so much proved to be a deep-fried paste of flour and water which had been cooked together. I think this recipe is the ultimate culinary attempt to make a silk purse out of a sow's ear.

Churros Madrilenos

(Crisp-fried Crullers)

2 cups water
1 teaspoon salt
2 cups flour
Vegetable oil for deep fat frying
Sugar

In a heavy saucepan, bring the water to a boil and add the salt. Remove the pan from the heat and dump in the flour all at once. Beat vigorously with a wooden spoon until the mixture forms a thick, coarse paste which pulls away from the sides of the pan. Cool it to room temperature (it may sit in a covered pan overnight).

Heat two inches of oil in a heavy skillet (an electric frying pan works perfectly) until it's very hot but not smoking (400°). Place the paste in a cookie press fitted with a star plate. Squeeze the dough into the hot fat, making each churros approximately four inches long. Fry until golden brown, turning once. Drain on paper towels. Coat the churros with granulated sugar by shaking in a bag containing sugar. Serve immediately.

Sometimes a really exquisite dish can be really simple to make. (Sometimes, but in reality it doesn't happen all that often). Tangerine granité has a marvelous flavor, is impressive to serve, and I'm sure it must be loaded with vitamin C. A granité, while not an igneous rock in this case, is a still-frozen sherbet. It can be served between courses of a dinner or as a dessert.

Tangerine Granité

1 tablespoon honey
2 cups fresh tangerine juice (juice from 10 to 12 tangerines), strained if desired
¼ teaspoon finely grated tangerine peel
1 ½ ounces orange-flavored liqueur (optional)

Dissolve the honey in a small amount of the juice in a 9×13 baking pan. Then add the remaining ingredients and stir until mixed. Freeze until solid or until ready to serve. (Do not stir!) When ready to serve, scrape the surface with a fork to break up ice crystals into a granular consistency. Serve immediately, garnished with tangerine sections. Makes eight servings.

Fresh orange juice, peel and sections can be used in the same proportions to make an orange granité.

HERE IS A PUDDING recipe that is almost as quick to make as stirring up a packaged brand and it has the added advantage of containing no artificial or modified food products. I might warn you that at first your children might think that this pudding tastes "different." It does, but it also tastes good!

If you have never made pudding "from scratch" and are wondering if it is necessary to go through the hocus pocus of adding a bit of the hot mixture to the eggs before adding the eggs to the remainder of the pudding, it is. This process gradually warms up the eggs and helps prevent them from coagulating into a solid lump when they are added to the very hot mixture in the pan. You might also want to know that two egg yolks may be substituted for one whole egg when making pudding.

Butterscotch Pudding

2 tablespoons butter
1 cup brown sugar
¼ teaspoon salt
3 cups milk
3 tablespoons flour
2 eggs
1 teaspoon vanilla

Melt the butter in a heavy saucepan. Add the sugar and salt and mix well. Slowly add 2 cups of the milk. Heat this to the boiling point.

Make a paste by adding the remaining 1 cup of milk to the flour. Add this to the boiling sugar mixture and cook, stirring constantly until it is thickened.

Beat the eggs in a small bowl. Add approximately ½ cup of the hot mixture to the eggs, and then add the egg mixture to the pudding. Cook for an additional 2 minutes and remove from the heat. Add the vanilla. Cool before serving.

Garnish with peanuts, whipped cream or sliced bananas, if desired. Makes 6–8 servings.

THERE ARE MANY PEOPLE who feel that an elaborate dessert can make up for any deficiency in the meal that precedes it. This may be true, but at a dinner party I prefer a light dessert, preferably one that can be made ahead of time, leaving the fancy dessert to be served when I am entertaining with "coffee and...." The following sherry soufflé is one of my favorite company desserts. If you don't have a soufflé dish, don't worry. Just make the soufflé in any serving dish and it will taste just as good. The eggs should be at room temperature for this recipe.

Sherry Soufflé

1 envelope unflavored gelatin
¾ cup sugar
⅛ teaspoon salt
4 pasteurized eggs, separated
½ cup water
½ cup cream sherry
1 cup heavy cream, whipped
Sweetened whipped cream (optional)
Maraschino cherries (optional)

In the top of a small double boiler, thoroughly mix together the gelatin, ¼ cup of the sugar and the salt. In a small bowl, blend together the egg yolks and water; stir into the gelatin mixture. Place the egg mixture over simmering (not boiling) water and cook, stirring constantly with a rubber spatula, until the gelatin is completely dissolved (about five minutes). Remove from the heat and stir in the sherry. Place the top of the double boiler over ice cubes and stir until the mixture is the consistency of unbeaten egg whites. Don't let it get too thick. Place the sherry mixture in a large bowl.

Beat the egg whites until foamy; gradually beat in the remaining ½ cup of sugar, continuing to beat until stiff but not dry. Gently fold the egg whites into the sherry mixture; then fold in the whipped cream. Turn into a 1 quart soufflé dish. Chill for several hours or overnight. Decorate the top with sweetened whipped cream and cherries if desired. Makes 6–8 small servings.

I like to accompany the sherry soufflé with a small rich cookie. My recipe for "petticoat tails" is a family and company favorite. (At Christmas time I roll the dough in red or green sugar before chilling.) These melt-in-the-mouth confections are a light version of Scotch shortbread. These cookies freeze well.

Petticoat Tails

1 ½ cups butter or margarine
1 cup powdered sugar
2 ½ cups flour
½ teaspoon salt
½ teaspoon soda
1 teaspoon vanilla

Mix all the ingredients together and beat until creamy. Chill until the dough is firm enough to form into rolls that are about one inch in diameter and 12 inches long. Wrap the rolls in waxed paper and chill them until firm. Slice thinly (approximately ⅛ inch thick) and bake on ungreased cookie sheets in a preheated 350° oven until firm. Makes about 90 cookies.

WHEN A RECIPE CALLS for sour cream, the proper thing to use is the commercial sour cream from the dairy case at the store. When milk or cream is pasteurized by heating it to about 145°, all the bacteria in the milk, including "the good ones," are killed. This is why pasteurized milk doesn't sour when left out at room temperature or held for a long period of time in the refrigerator. Instead, airborne bacteria settle in it and cause it to spoil, instead of becoming thick and tart tasting.

Commercial sour cream is made by culturing light cream (18–20 percent butterfat) with Streptococcus lactis at 72° for about 15 hours before it is packaged. If you want to make your own sour cream, you can mix two cups of light cream with five tablespoons of commercial buttermilk and let the mixture sit at room temperature for 24 hours. The sour cream will improve in taste if refrigerated for 24 hours before using.

Here is a recipe for some very good sour cream gingerbread. I served it with whipped cream that I hadn't used up during the holiday season, but it would also be good served with applesauce or ice cream.

This moist, heavy gingerbread keeps exceptionally well.

Spicy Sour Cream Gingerbread

2 eggs
½ cup sour cream
½ cup molasses
½ cup brown sugar
1 ½ cups flour
1 teaspoon baking soda
1 teaspoon ginger
½ teaspoon cinnamon
¼ teaspoon powdered cloves
¼ teaspoon grated nutmeg
¼ teaspoon salt
½ cup melted butter or margarine

Beat the eggs well. Add the sour cream, molasses and brown sugar, and again beat well. Sift or stir together the flour, baking soda, ginger, cinnamon, cloves, nutmeg and salt, and stir this dry mixture into the egg mixture. Add the melted butter and mix well. Pour the batter into a well greased 8 or 9 inch square pan and bake in a preheated 350° oven for 30 minutes. Serve either warm or cold. Serves nine.

Several years ago, M.K.F. Fischer wrote an article on foods which bring comfort. Her own personal favorite was a simple dish of homemade applesauce, which evoked memories of childhood and her mother.

The other day I offered to share my lunch with my husband. He took one look at what I was preparing and said, "I don't feel up to milk toast." I explained to him that one didn't feel "up to" milk toast; one felt "down to" it. To me a slice or two of fresh buttered toast placed in a bowl and then covered with hot milk and sprinkled with a little salt is a comforting food. It is warm, it has memories associated with childhood and my mother's care, it always tastes pretty much the same, and I never have to worry about how it might settle on a somewhat queasy stomach.

While you may not want to serve milk toast, you might want to make another of my favorite comfort foods, baked custard. Custard doesn't have to be served as a dessert. It also makes a good breakfast treat or even a whole meal for those who don't feel much like eating.

Baked Custard

3 cups milk
3 eggs or 6 egg yolks
½ cup sugar (to taste)
¼ teaspoon salt
1 teaspoon vanilla
Nutmeg (optional)

Scald the milk by heating it in a small saucepan until bubbles just appear around the edge of the pan; heating the milk helps the custard cook more quickly and be tenderer. Set aside.

In a medium-sized bowl, beat the eggs just enough to blend them evenly. Stir in the desired amount of sugar and salt. Slowly add the hot milk while stirring continually. Add the vanilla and stir again. Divide the custard among six buttered custard cups and sprinkle with nutmeg, if desired. Place the cups in a shallow pan on a folded paper towel (so they won't rattle). Add about one inch of hot water to the pan.

Bake in a preheated 325° oven for about one hour. If you are using the oven for something else at the same time, the custard may also be baked at 350° for about 45 minutes. Test for doneness by inserting a knife tip near the edge of one cup. If it comes out clean, the custard is done and will be firm when cool. The custard may also be baked in a large dish. Serves six.

ONE OF THE HIGHLIGHTS of a recent trip was the time I spent at Joe Cahn's New Orleans School of Cooking, which convenes daily to teach tourists the joys of gumbo, jambalaya and other Creole delicacies.

Cahn, a jovial native of the city, began his class by telling of the first skirmish of the women's liberation movement, which occurred in New Orleans in the 1720s. It seems the young ladies who had been sent from France to become brides of the early settlers descended upon the governor's home, demanding to be sent back home because there was no food fit to cook in the new colony.

Since the governor couldn't afford to send the young ladies home, he sent his capable housekeeper to live with the Indians in order to discover what they ate. She came back and taught the women how to cook native fish and game and season them with wild herbs and grasses. That was the beginning of Creole cooking. When the Spanish came in the 1760s, they brought sugar cane and peppers to help season the regional cuisine, enhancing the use of what was available locally. Slaves from Africa soon were working in the kitchens and adding their contributions.

To me the most fascinating part of the class was the preparation of a bread pudding which was completely different from any I had ever tasted. Usually bread pudding is a custard with bread added to make it go farther. Creole bread pudding is a completely different animal—the bread is the most important ingredient. The pudding is made with completely dry bread so that every bit of custard is soaked up, and the finished product is solid and chock full of good things. It is not a dainty dish, but is a delicious one that appears on the menus of the finest restaurants in New Orleans.

Cahn's basic formula is six to eight cups of dry bread, four cups of liquid, four tablespoons of butter and three eggs. The bread can be anything you want—French, whole wheat, stale Danish or even chocolate chip cookies, each making a different delicious pudding. How would you like a pudding made with chocolate milk and studded with M&M's or a piña colada pudding using coconut cream as part of the four cups of liquid, along with pineapple and rum? The possible combinations seem endless.

This is a no-fuss recipe. Since it makes 16 to 20 servings, it is good to know that it freezes well. Cahn recommends freezing with the sauce already on it, so all you have to do is thaw, warm it and eat.

Joe Cahn's New Orleans Bread Pudding

1 ten oz loaf of stale French bread (6–8 cups of any dry bread)
4 cups milk
2 cups sugar
4 tablespoons butter, melted
3 eggs
1 teaspoon nutmeg
2 tablespoons vanilla
1 cup raisins
1 cup coconut
1 cup chopped pecans
1 teaspoon cinnamon

Combine all the ingredients in a large bowl and stir them around until the dry bread has absorbed the liquid; the mixture should be very moist but not soupy. Pour into a buttered 9×9 inch baking dish and place in a cold oven. Bake at 350° for approximately 1 hour and 15 minutes or until the top is golden brown. Serve warm with sauce. Serves sixteen to twenty.

Whiskey Sauce

½ cup butter
1 ½ cups powdered sugar
1 egg or 1 egg yolk
¼ cup bourbon (to taste) or fruit juice

Cream the butter and sugar together in a small sauce pan over medium heat until all of the butter is absorbed. Remove from the heat and blend in the egg. Add the bourbon gradually, stirring constantly. The sauce will thicken as it cools. Serve the warm sauce over warm bread pudding. For a variety of sauces, just substitute your favorite fruit juice or liquor to complement the pudding.

ALONG WITH BRIGHTLY COLORED leaves and beautiful blue skies, Minnesota apples herald the change of season. There have been locally grown apples available at the Farmers' Market for about a month now, and every week seems to bring new varieties. My favorites are the Minjons, which are an excellent eating apple and also produce beautiful pink applesauce.

Two of my favorite ways of serving apples, other than just polished to a shiny red perfection, is with creamy brie cheese or fried with a bit of butter and sugar. The other day I served apple slices and brie with a hearty chicken soup, which was chock-full of carrots, celery, shallots and little buttery dumplings. It was an excellent dinner, and we ate twice as many apples as I had originally prepared.

I make fried apples by coring and thinly slicing about one and a half apples per person; they shrink when cooked. I put a generous gob of butter in a small frying pan and sauté the apples until they are just soft. Then I add sugar to taste and raise the heat under the pan and cook until the slices are coated with a light buttery glaze. They are particularly good with pork. If you like, the apples can be seasoned with a bit of cinnamon and/or nutmeg, but I like the flavor of the buttery apples without any dressing up.

Another apple favorite is an apple sundae. You coarsely chop one tart, firm eating apple per person and top it with warm caramel sauce. I suppose you could put a scoop of vanilla ice cream under the apple and top the whole thing with toasted, slivered almonds, but it certainly isn't necessary. You can use a prepared hot caramel sauce if you don't want to fuss with sticky pans, or you can quickly stir up your own while making dinner.

This recipe calls for cream; whole milk can be substituted for the cream if you realize that the finished sauce will not be as rich. Chocolate chips work fine in the recipe.

Chocolate Caramel Sauce

4 ounces semi-sweet chocolate or ¾ cup chocolate chips
1 cup brown sugar
½ cup cream
1 tablespoon butter
1 teaspoon vanilla

In a small saucepan, melt the chocolate over low heat. Then stir in the brown sugar, cream and butter, and continue cooking until the sauce is the desired thickness. Remove from the heat and cool slightly before adding the vanilla. Serve warm. Makes about 1 cup of sauce.

When I had breakfast at a Minneapolis restaurant recently, I had a delicious compote of dried fruits which was served with a bit of crème fraîche on the top. With a croissant and a cup of café au lait, it made an elegant beginning to the day.

Crème fraîche is a rich French sour cream made from unpastuerized cream. It is a classic accompaniment to fresh berries. You can easily make the American version of crème fraîche by mixing together one cup of whipping cream and two and a half tablespoons of commercial buttermilk or sour cream and then let it sit at room temperature up to twenty-four hours, until it is thick. Crème fraîche can withstand higher temperatures in cooking without curdling than sour cream can.

Here also is a recipe for dried fruits in port which I think goes the restaurant compote that I had one better, by adding a few nuts for additional flavor and texture. It could be served at either end of a meal, as an appetizer or as a dessert. Since I really don't care for raisins, I have listed them as optional. But if you like them, use as many as you think taste good. And remember, a co-op is a good place to buy small amounts of dried fruits and nuts.

Crème Fraîche

1 cup whipping cream
2 ½ tablespoons buttermilk

Place the whipping cream and the buttermilk in a clean glass jar. Mix well and then cover tightly. Let the mixture stand at room temperature (about 70°) for from 8 to 24 hours, or until very thick. Refrigerate until ready to use. Crème fraîche may be stored in the refrigerator for up to 10 days.

Winter Fruits In Port

¼ cup pitted prunes
¼ cup pecan halves
½ cup dried apricots
¼ cup raisins (optional)
¼ cup whole blanched almonds
¼ cup pitted dates
2 tablespoons sugar
1 cup port wine
½ stick cinnamon
1 whole clove

Place the prunes in the bottom of a glass pint container. Add the pecans, apricots, raisins, almonds and dates in layers. Combine the sugar, port wine, cinnamon and clove in a small saucepan and heat until the sugar has dissolved and the mixture is hot, but not boiling. Immediately pour over the fruit. When cool, cover and refrigerate until ready to use. Serves four.

SOME RECIPES REALLY ARE simpler than others to make. It isn't always necessary to spend hours in the kitchen in order to produce something that will impress your guests or family because it tastes so good.

Here is a recipe for the Italian dessert called tortoni, which is simply frozen, sweetened ricotta cheese. The recipe calls for almond extract and ground almonds, but if you want to serve the dessert topped with sliced fresh strawberries or some other fresh fruit, you can substitute one teaspoon of vanilla for the almond extract and omit the ground almonds. Or you can stir in a quarter of a cup of coarsely grated semi-sweet chocolate in the vanilla-flavored mixture for a nice texture and taste combination. Or if you are one of those people who puts aside recipes for Christmas entertaining, you could make the tortoni with almond extract and stir in a quarter of a cup of finely chopped red and green candied fruit.

If you like to use honey as a natural sweetener, substitute a quarter of a cup of honey for the sugar listed in the recipe.

Tortoni

1 pound ricotta cheese (about 2 cups)
⅓ cup sugar
1 teaspoon almond extract
6–8 teaspoons finely ground almonds

Whip the ricotta cheese, sugar and almond extract together until the mixture is light and fluffy. Line a muffin tin with six to eight paper liners, or place six to eight small paper cups in a pan, and divide the mixture among them. Sprinkle each with 1 teaspoon of ground almonds. Freeze. Allow the tortoni to stand at room temperature for about 15 minutes before serving, so that they will soften slightly. Serves six to eight.

If you are not going to use all the tortoni very soon, remove them from the pan and wrap for freezer storage.

CHOOSING A RESTAURANT IN a strange city is always something of an adventure. On a Monday night in Florence, it was my turn and I chose Restaurante Natale, which was said to have one of the best kitchens in town. It proved to be a wonderful choice. The food was delicious, and the restaurant was pleasant with its wrought iron chandeliers adorned with dragons and its walls covered with old photographs of the city. But perhaps best of all were the friendly people who operate the restaurant.

We had such a good time at Restaurante Natale that we decided to eat there again on Wednesday and sample some different items. Jerry had a lovely dish of calf liver sliced very thin and served in an onion sauce made by cooking sliced onions until they were reduced to a pulp and then stirring them into the pan juices. I tried the osso bucco, even though it isn't a Tuscan specialty, because I wanted to see how it compared with the osso bucco I make when I can find veal shanks. It was excellent.

By this time our waiter felt free enough to ask me about my little green notebook and why I took notes while I was eating. I told him that I write a column for our local newspaper and that I would write about the places we had been and the food we had eaten when we got home. This led to an invitation to come to the restaurant the next morning to watch him make a dessert whose recipe I could share. This was an invitation I couldn't refuse.

Here is the recipe for the dessert, Zuppa Florentina, a rich, delicious uncooked egg crème, as I worked it out in my kitchen. I used vanilla wafers in place of the biscotti, but you must dunk them into the coffee very quickly or they will turn to mush before you can put them into the serving bowl. Do a small handful at a time. The recipe calls for espresso. If you don't have an espresso machine, you could use an instant espresso mix to make the coffee, or perhaps you could even use a strong version of your favorite coffee.

Since the Italian cheese was softer and richer than our cream cheese, I substituted eight ounces of cream cheese whipped with ¼ cup of heavy cream. Sugar affects how quickly egg whites whip. If you are whipping the whites with a whisk, follow the directions below, but if you are whipping the eggs with a mixer, you might want to add the sugar gradually, beating well after each addition so that you don't over beat them. I found that my baking cocoa was lumpy enough that it needed sifting. I also found that the dessert could be frozen overnight and still retain its original consistency when thawed for about 1 ½ hours before serving.

Zuppa Florentina

8 pasteurized eggs, separated
8 ounces cream cheese
¼ cup heavy cream
One 11 ounce package vanilla wafers
4 cups espresso
1 ¼ cups sugar
4 tablespoons dry cocoa

Have all of the ingredients at room temperature. With a whisk beat the egg whites until they are stiff, but not dry. Stir in the slightly beaten egg yolks and the cream cheese, which has already been whipped with the heavy cream.

Quickly dip the vanilla wafers in the coffee and divide between 2 bowls. (I used 7 and 8 inch soufflé dishes.) Add the sugar to the egg mixture and mix well. Divide about ⅔ of the egg crème between the bowls and sprinkle each with 1 tablespoon of cocoa. Carefully spoon in the remainder of the crème and top each bowl with an additional tablespoon of cocoa. Place in the freezer for about an hour. Remove from the freezer about 15 minutes before serving. Serves twelve to sixteen.

I THINK THAT I could easily turn into a fruititerian, if there is such an animal. I rejoice in the cherries, grapes, plums, peaches and nectarines which are now available in the markets. I delight in their tastes, textures and smells. But most of all, I enjoy the small wild strawberries which grow in my yard and the wonderful juicy raspberries which my neighbor shares with me.

This bounty of summer reminds me of a cartoon which is posted on my refrigerator. It shows a little girl biting into a big apple; the caption reads, "Ummm! This is a good recipe!"

The best recipe for many fruits is to just enjoy them as they are. When we were in Italy last summer, even the most elegant restaurants offered a bowl of perfect raspberries or tiny wild strawberries as the equal to the most elaborate pastries and confections. But sometimes it is fun to use this bounty in cooking, either because we are tired of plain fruit, or the occasion seems to demand something more elaborate, or we need to stretch the amount of fruit we have available.

Here is a recipe for an old-fashioned berry Bavarian cream, which is once again beginning to appear on the menus of good restaurants and which serves all three of these reasons. The recipe can be made with either strawberries or raspberries. If you make it with raspberries, you may wish to sieve out some of the seeds. If you use strawberries, you may want to add a tablespoon of fresh lemon juice to the gelatin mixture to pick up the flavor of the berries. The mixture may also be placed in a baked pie shell for an elegant chiffon pie.

Berry Bavarian Cream

1 quart berries
½–1 cup sugar (to taste)
2 teaspoons gelatin
3 tablespoons cold water
3 tablespoons boiling water
1 tablespoon lemon juice (optional)
1 cup whipping cream
Additional fruit for garnish

Clean and hull the fruit if necessary. Crush the fruit, add the sugar and let the mixture stand at least 30 minutes. Sieve to remove seeds if desired. In a cup, soak the gelatin in the cold water to soften; then dissolve it by adding the boiling water. Stir the gelatin solution into the berries, adding lemon juice if desired. Chill the mixture until it just begins to set. Whip the cream and fold it gently into the berry mixture.

Pour the Bavarian cream into a wet mold or into 6–8 attractive glasses. Chill until firm, for 12 hours if you plan to unmold it. Garnish with additional fruit. Serves six to eight.

THIS FRESH-TASTING DESSERT, which is known in my family as Snow Pudding, makes a delightful ending to a summer dinner. It is possible to cheat and use a small package of lemon Jell-O and produce a good dessert, but making your own fresh lemon-gelatin mixture will make an even better one. With the growing interest in comfort foods, this recipe deserves to be better known.

Swedish Snow Pudding

1 envelope unflavored gelatin
¼ cup cold water
1 cup boiling water
½–¾ cup sugar
¼ cup lemon juice
1 tablespoon grated lemon rind
3 pasteurized egg whites, stiffly beaten
½ pint whipping cream, whipped
Sauce

Soak the gelatin in the cold water for five minutes to soften. Add the boiling water and stir until the gelatin is dissolved. Stir in the sugar, lemon juice and rind. Chill the gelatin mixture until it is the consistency of unbeaten egg whites; then beat it until it is frothy. Fold in the pasteurized egg whites and whipped cream. Turn into a serving dish or individual molds. Chill overnight, well covered. Serve the raspberry sauce over the pudding. Serves eight to twelve, or two to three nostalgic Swedes.

Raspberry Sauce

1 twelve ounce package frozen raspberries
½ to 1 cup sugar
2 tablespoons butter
2 tablespoons cornstarch

Place the raspberries, sugar and butter in a sauce pan and cook them until the sugar is dissolved and the butter melted. Remove about ¼ cup of juice from the raspberry mixture and stir the cornstarch into it, mixing thoroughly. Add this cornstarch mixture to the berries and cook slowly, stirring occasionally, until the mixture thickens. Cool and chill before serving.

Hors d'Oeuvres

Corner Bar   P. Lampe

When I am having a dinner party, I usually serve some good cheese and crackers as the hors d'oeuvre. I would rather concentrate on what I am going to serve for dinner. But there are occasions when it is nice to have a selection of hors d'oeuvres. If they can be made ahead of time, so much the better. The first recipe is one of my husband's favorites. It is very easy to make. You can use either canned or frozen crab, although I prefer the frozen. The second is a recipe for a reliable appetizer, which can be made well ahead of time.

Chili Cheese And Crab

1 (12 ounce) bottle chili sauce
8 ounces cream cheese, softened
3–4 ounces crab meat
¼ cup parsley, chopped
Melba toast

In a shallow serving dish, place the softened cream cheese in a layer and top it with the chili sauce. Sprinkle parsley on top of the sauce. Top with the drained, picked-over crab. Serve with Melba toast rounds. Help yourself first, scooping down into the cheese so that your guests will realize what is underneath.

Florentine Spread

1 package frozen, chopped spinach (10 ounces)
1 hard-cooked egg
1 can water chestnuts (8 ounces)
4 slices crisp-cooked bacon
¼ cup minced green onions
¼ teaspoon garlic salt
½ teaspoon salt
1 cup plain yogurt
Melba toast or crackers

Drain the spinach thoroughly, pressing with the back of a spoon to remove excess moisture. Finely chop the hard-cooked egg and drained water chestnuts and crumble the bacon. In a medium-sized bowl, mix together the spinach, egg, water chestnuts, bacon, green onions, salts and yogurt. Refrigerate until serving time. Serve with Melba toast or crackers. Makes three cups.

IF YOU FOUND YOURSELF in a Swiss mountain hut at suppertime and all that you could find in the cupboard were a bit of wine, a couple of pieces of cheese and some halfway stale bread, what could you make of it? The answer of course is cheese fondue.

Cheese fondue is another example of a basically peasant food being elevated to the level of haute cuisine. Its chief merits are that it's fun to make, fun to eat and filling.

Several years ago fondue was very fashionable. Kitchenware departments were full of equipment and I'm sure many marriages started with enough pots, burners, forks and cute nutmeg graters to last a lifetime. But fashions change, and many fondue sets are gathering dust on a back shelf of the top cupboard or are in the box destined for the next garage sale. Well dust it off and serve fondue to your family some night. It doesn't have to be a party. It has become one of my family's favorite change-of-pace dinners.

Cheese fondue is best made with *real* Swiss cheese, and we are lucky to have it readily available here. American Swiss cheese tastes fine, but isn't aged as long as that the Swiss make and therefore tends to form strings when heated. It is best to cut the cheese into small cubes instead of grating it, as grated cheese tends to form clots and lumps when added to a hot liquid. I prefer to use a mixture of half Emmentaler and half Gruyère cheese.

It is best to use a young dry wine of the Rhine, Moselle, or Chablis type. If you are worried about your children consuming wine, remember that all the alcohol is evaporated before the fondue is ready to eat. You may omit the finishing touch of brandy or kirsch if you desire.

If you do not have an efficient alcohol burner, you may cook the fondue in the kitchen and then keep it warm at the table on a hot tray or over a candle warmer.

Remember that each bite-sized cube of bread should have crust on at least one side to give it strength so it won't crumble when dipped into the cheese mixture.

The Swiss prefer to drink something warm when eating fondue; tea is typical. Hot cider would also be good. Fondue is a meal in itself. Crisp apples would make a good ending to the meal.

Cheese Fondue

1 pound Swiss cheese (½ Emmentaler, ½ Gruyère)
1½ tablespoons cornstarch
1 clove garlic
2 cups dry white wine
3 tablespoons kirsch or brandy
Nutmeg and pepper to taste
2 loaves French bread cut into bite-sized cubes

Cut the cheese into small cubes and dredge them with corn starch. Rub the cooking pot with the split clove of garlic. Add the wine and set over a moderate heat. When bubbles begin to rise to the surface, start to add the cheese by small handfuls, stirring constantly with a wooden spoon until the cheese is all melted. Add the kirsch or brandy and spices, continuing stirring until blended. Serve and keep the fondue bubbling over a burner. Spear the bread cubes through the soft part into the crust and dunk in the fondue. Serves four to six.

It is the time of year when you begin to think of the entertaining you would like to do. This might range from an evening of video games to a sit-down dinner. Beer and pretzels might serve as refreshments for the first occasion, but for the latter you would like to serve something special, yet not too difficult to make. Here is a bit of encouragement to go ahead and actually issue invitations to that dinner party.

Experts always say that you should try out your recipes before serving them to company. I think this is the biggest stumbling block to entertaining that there is. In many cases, a party recipe produces too much, at too great a price, of something that the younger members of your family will probably turn up their noses at.

If you like all the ingredients in a recipe and are familiar with the techniques called for, you will produce something that tastes good. If you are still timid, stick to a tried and true recipe for your main course but experiment with the befores and afters. This recipe can be served informally either as an hors d'oeuvre or as an appetizer at the table.

Home-Pickled Halibut

1 pound halibut, thawed if necessary
¾ cup water
¾ cup white vinegar
¼ cup white wine
¼ cup sugar
1 teaspoon salt, or to taste
2 teaspoons olive oil
1 bay leaf
5 peppercorns
4 cloves
1 small onion, thinly sliced
1 lemon, thinly sliced

Remove the skin and bones from the halibut and cut it into 1 inch pieces. In a large saucepan combine the water, vinegar, wine, sugar, salt, oil, bay leaf, peppercorns and cloves. Bring the liquid to a boil; add the halibut pieces and simmer gently for 3 to 5 minutes or until the halibut barely flakes when tested with a fork. Don't overcook. Layer the halibut pieces, onion and lemon in a serving bowl and pour the stock over all. Refrigerate, covered, overnight. Drain before serving. Serves eight.

If you have some left-over turkey on hand, you might want to freeze some of it and then resurrect it for this pâté, which could be served at a holiday party.

Turkey Pâté

½ cup finely-chopped carrot
½ cup finely-chopped celery
⅓ cup finely-chopped onion
2 tablespoons oil
⅓ cup dry white wine
1 teaspoon salt
2 teaspoons dill weed
1 teaspoon capers, chopped
3 cups ground turkey
½ cup chopped almonds
2 hard-cooked eggs, chopped

Cook the carrot, celery and onion in the oil until tender. Remove from the heat and stir in the remaining ingredients; process the mixture in four batches until smooth in either a food processor or a blender. Pour the pâté into an oiled 4 cup mold and chill until ready to serve. Unmold and serve with a variety of crackers or thin toasted slices of French bread.

According to the Chinese calendar this is the Year of the Boar, and I have a charming poster of a smiling pig to remind me that this is to be a year of prosperity for everyone who savors the joys of living.

The Chinese lunar calendar is divided into twelve terrestrial branches each symbolized by an animal. The boar is the last of these symbolic animals and represents the bounty that man has built up over past years. The Chinese feel that this should be a year to reflect and enjoy the fruits of your labors.

People born in the Year of the Boar (1911, 1923, 1935, 1947, 1959, 1971, 1983, 1995...) are supposed to share the characteristics the Chinese attribute to the pig. They are intellectuals with a thirst for knowledge. They are gallant and chivalrous, sensitive and innocent. Their diligence and aptitude for hard work leads to success in their chosen careers.

Besides all this the pig has to be the symbol of much which is good in Chinese cuisine. Pigs are reported to have been domesticated in China as far back as 5000 B.C. Today China is the leading hog-producing country in the world. It is said that a good Chinese cook knows how to use every part of the pig, including the squeal.

One of the great joys of the San Francisco area is the number of Chinese restaurants available. When we lived in Berkeley, we settled on a favorite—the Hang Ah Tea Room—and slowly managed to sample a goodly portion of its menu. The dim sum which was available at lunch time with unending variety is probably impossible to recreate in a Western kitchen.

However, I do have a recipe for a very good dim sum or hors d'oeuvre using ground pork.

If you lack a Chinese steamer, the mushrooms may be placed on a plate and covered with a double thickness of waxed paper. The plate then can be placed on a rack or on two inverted cups in a roaster containing an inch of water. The recipe calls for two inch mushrooms, but if you want to serve them as finger food, you might want to use smaller ones.

Pork Stuffed Mushrooms

10 large mushrooms, 2 inch
½ pound ground pork
½ pound shrimp, minced
4 water chestnuts, chopped
2 tablespoons cornstarch
½ teaspoon salt
1 teaspoon sugar
2 tablespoons soy sauce
Parsley (optional)

Clean the mushrooms, pat dry and remove their stems. Mix together the pork, shrimp, chestnuts, cornstarch, salt, sugar and soy sauce. Stuff the mushrooms with the mixture and place them on a heat-proof plate. Cover with double thickness of waxed paper. Steam for 40 minutes. Serve hot.

Our summer-like weather continues to give us a supply of fresh, locally-grown vegetables which can make good "befores." I define a "before" as sort of an informal hors d'oeuvre, the type of thing you might set out on the kitchen counter to tide the kids over until dinner or even to quench your hunger pangs until the meal is cooked. Of course, they can also be served at a party. Apple slices topped with a little cheese, raw vegetables with a good dip or tastily spread crackers are all good "befores."

Here is a recipe for a spinach sour cream dip which is especially good with fresh raw vegetables, although it may also be served with chips or crackers. A thawed package of frozen spinach may be substituted for the fresh spinach.

Spinach Dip

10 ounces fresh spinach
¼ cup parsley, finely minced
1 small onion, minced
2 tablespoons lemon juice
1 tablespoon white wine vinegar
¼ cup mayonnaise
1 cup sour cream
Salt and pepper to taste

Wash the spinach. Place the spinach including its stems, with only the water clinging to the leaves, in a large sauce pan. Cook uncovered over moderate heat until the spinach is wilted, turning the spinach over several times with a spoon while it is cooking. Transfer the spinach to a colander and hold it under running water until it is completely cool. Drain well, wrap in a kitchen towel, and squeeze to remove as much moisture as possible. Chop the spinach finely (this may be done in a blender or food processor). Add the parsley, onion, lemon juice, vinegar, mayonnaise and sour cream; mix well. Taste to see if it needs salt and pepper. Serve with crudités—raw carrots, turnips, kohlrabi, cucumbers, beets, mushrooms, zucchini, broccoli, cherry tomatoes, etc.

Eggplant caviar is a classic Middle Eastern spread. It is good served on toasted pita bread or crackers or with crudités. I also like it as an unusual topping for hamburgers.

Eggplant Caviar

1 large eggplant (1 pound)
1 cup parsley, minced
1 large clove garlic, peeled and minced
1 small piece onion, minced
½ cup mayonnaise
½ teaspoon basil
½ teaspoon oregano
½ teaspoon dill weed
2 teaspoons lemon juice
Salt and pepper to taste

Preheat oven to 300°. Bake the whole eggplant on a cookie sheet for 50 minutes or until it is completely softened. Cool, cut into quarters and peel. Puree the eggplant; use a blender, food processor, food mill or potato masher. Stir in the parsley, garlic, onion, mayonnaise, basil, dill, oregano and lemon juice, mixing thoroughly. Taste and add desired amount of salt and pepper. Refrigerate several hours before serving.

Several weeks ago at a party a friend, who happens to bear a fine old Norwegian name, gently chided me for the lack of Norwegian recipes in this column. He assured me that given the ethnic makeup of our community many people are interested in Norwegian cooking. I found that, reflecting my background, I have lots of Swedish recipes, quite a few Danish recipes and some which are vaguely labeled Scandinavian, but very few that bear a Norwegian label. I did find a nice recipe for roast reindeer with goat-cheese sauce; however, I have never seen a haunch of reindeer in our local stores.

I will use a recipe for Norwegian meatballs, which I found in *The New York Times International Cookbook,* and which seems to be identical with my Swedish meatball recipe. My friend assured me that his wife made the best Norwegian meatballs and seasoned them with mace. You might want to try that addition or substitution in this recipe. Mace is an interesting spice. It is the fibrous husk around nutmegs, somewhat like the husk that grows around a black walnut. The large evergreen, *Myristica fragrans,* which grows in New Guinea and Indonesia, is the only plant I know which bears two distinct spices.

This recipe uses both mashed potatoes and bread crumbs to extend the meat and ensure that the meatballs will be moist as well as flavorful. Try substituting ½ teaspoon mace for the nutmeg and allspice.

Norwegian Meatballs

1 pound extra-lean ground beef
½ pound ground pork
1 egg, slightly beaten
½ cup mashed potatoes
½ cup dry bread crumbs
½ cup milk
1 teaspoon salt
¼ teaspoon ground cloves
¼ teaspoon allspice
¼ teaspoon ground ginger
¼ teaspoon pepper
¼ teaspoon nutmeg
½ teaspoon brown sugar
Flour
2 tablespoons oil
2 tablespoons butter
1 cup heavy cream

Combine the meats, egg, potatoes, bread crumbs, milk, salt, spices and brown sugar. Blend them well and shape the mixture into 24 meatballs. Roll the balls in flour.

Heat the oil and butter in a large frying pan and brown the meatballs on all sides. Spoon the balls into an oven-proof casserole and pour the cream over them. Set the casserole in a large pan and pour boiling water around it. Cover the casserole and bake for 40 minutes in a preheated 325° oven. Serves six.

WE RECENTLY CELEBRATED OUR wedding anniversary by going out to dinner with friends who were married on the same day we were. I started my meal with a tomato bruschetta because I wanted to see what the restaurant could do with this Roman-style antipasto. The dish turned out to be a very attractive pinwheel of toasted garlic bread topped with a generous portion of diced tomatoes, good olive oil and fresh basil. It was a hearty peasant dish of bread and oil, transformed by the addition of the tomatoes, garlic, basil and freshly ground pepper into a dish which could be served as an antipasto, as a salad or even as a luncheon entree.

The important thing when making bruschetta is to start with good quality ingredients: good solid bread and a fresh heavy green olive oil. Here is my version of tomato bruschetta.

Tomato Bruschetta

**3 baggette slices, 1 inch wide, cut diagonally and
   halved horizontally**
1 clove garlic, peeled and lightly crushed
1 fresh tomato, diced and drained
1 teaspoon chopped fresh basil
1–2 tablespoons good quality olive oil
Freshly ground pepper

Toast the bread under the broiler on both sides until it is golden brown. Immediately rub the cut side of the toast with garlic. Arrange the toast on a warm serving plate and top it with the tomato and basil. Drizzle the olive oil over it. Season with pepper. Serve immediately. Serves one.

Meats

Carleton Chapel   P. Lampe

CHUCK ROAST HAS BEEN on special at the supermarkets the last couple of weeks. When I was growing up, chuck roast was synonymous with pot roast, cooked with potatoes, carrots and possibly a bit of onion—an all-American dish but alas, not a very exciting one.

This recipe is for pot roast in a very zippy sauce. Serve it with buttered noodles to which you have added a few poppy seeds or with couscous, also a green vegetable or salad, and some crisp bread or a hard roll, and you will have an excellent autumn dinner. The bread is an important part of this meal because the sauce is so good you will need something to wipe your plate clean.

Any leftovers can be cut into small pieces, heated up, and served with lots of sauce on a Kaiser roll to make one of the best and sloppiest sandwiches I have ever eaten.

Tasty Pot Roast

3 ½ pound chuck roast
1 large onion, chopped
1 ½ cups beef broth
½ cup catsup
3 tablespoons soy sauce
2 tablespoons Worcestershire sauce
2 tablespoons prepared mustard
2 tablespoons cornstarch
2 tablespoons water

Brown the meat in a large frying pan. Remove the meat and brown the onions in the same pan. Add the beef broth (if using canned broth, dilute it to regular strength), catsup, soy sauce, Worcestershire sauce and mustard. Stir to blend. Return the meat to the pan and cook it covered in a 350° oven for 2 ½ hours. Remove meat from the pan, skim off excess fat and thicken the sauce with the cornstarch dissolved in the water. Bring the sauce to a boil over medium heat while stirring constantly. Simmer for a couple of minutes and serve immediately. Serves four to six.

MANY YEARS AGO I worked in a laboratory with a charming doctor of Greek heritage whose name was Agamemnon Despopoulis. Ag was many things: physician, teacher, researcher, father of a fine family. But he was also a cook.

He shared with me his formula for a simple barbecue sauce: ⅓ catsup, ⅓ soy sauce, ⅓ sherry, plus whatever else you might want to add to jazz it up a bit, such as garlic, Tabasco sauce, green pepper, or onions. I have used this sauce with ribs and grilled chicken, but my favorite use is in what I like to call Gourmet Sloppy Joes.

Gourmet Sloppy Joes

1 large onion, thinly sliced
1 ½ pound ground beef
⅓ cup catsup
⅓ cup soy sauce
⅓ cup sherry
Salt and pepper

Sauté the onion in a small amount of oil until soft, but not brown. Remove it from the skillet and cook the ground beef in the remaining oil until done. Remove any excess fat from the pan and add the onion, catsup, soy sauce and sherry. Simmer for 15 minutes. Serve on a toasted bun. Makes 6 to 8 sandwiches.

Stir frying is an Oriental cooking technique which has become very popular over the past few years. It consists of cooking small pieces of food in a little bit of oil over high heat. The food is tossed and turned continually and cooks in a very short period of time. This method of cooking probably evolved as a means of saving fuel.

The traditional pan used for stir frying is the round bottomed wok, which allows you to push the cooked pieces of food up on the side of the pan while you continue frying the rest of the food in the hot bottom portion of the wok. If you don't have a wok, a heavy frying pan can be used.

While stir fried food has to be cooked just before serving, much of the preparation can be done beforehand. The meat can be sliced and marinated, if necessary; the vegetables peeled and diced or sliced; the rest of the ingredients gathered. Stir fried dishes can be very creative. It is easy to vary the ingredients to suit your taste or to fit what you have available.

Steak, onions and tomatoes is a favorite American combination that can be adapted to stir frying. I use a thick piece of top round, or family steak. If the meat is partially frozen, it is possible to slice it very thinly.

Beef with Tomatoes and Onions

1 pound round steak
4 tablespoons dry sherry
4 teaspoons soy sauce
1 teaspoon sugar
2 teaspoons cornstarch
White of one small egg
2 cloves garlic
2 slices fresh ginger
1 large yellow onion
½ pound ripe tomatoes (probably two)

Slice the meat as thinly as possible. Combine the slices with 1 tablespoon sherry, 2 teaspoons soy sauce, the sugar, 1 teaspoon cornstarch, and the egg white. Refrigerate at least 30 minutes. Mince together the garlic and ginger. Slice the onion and dice the tomatoes. Combine the remaining sherry, soy sauce and cornstarch.

Place about two tablespoons of oil in the wok or pan and heat. When hot, add the garlic and ginger and cook a few seconds. Add the beef mixture and stir fry over high heat until browned, about two to three minutes. Remove the meat from the wok and set it aside.

Wipe out the wok, add one tablespoon of oil and stir fry the onions for two minutes. Add the tomatoes and stir fry another minute. Add the sherry, soy sauce, starch mixture and heat until thickened. Add the beef and stir. Serve immediately. Serves four.

In the late 1970s a new type of pea seed appeared in the seed catalogues. It was the result of crossing a regular snow pea with a one-in-a-million mutant shell pea plant. The resultant plants bore sweet, juicy, crunchy peas with edible pods. They were named sugar snap peas. The plants grow six to eight feet tall and produce lots of peapods. When the peas were first introduced, you had to grow your own, but sugar snap peas now appear at the Farmers' Market and on the produce counters of supermarkets.

One of the most delightful ways to eat this vegetable is raw—just wash, remove their strings and eat them. They have strings along both sides of the pods that must be removed. If you want to be a little fancier, serve them whole with your favorite dip.

You can also try stringing the pea pods, shelling the peas, and saving the pods to dip in a mixture made by puréeing the peas and adding them to a cup of your favorite dip, pepped up with ¼ teaspoon of ground ginger and a teaspoon of Worcestershire sauce. Store the pods in plastic bags in the refrigerator until ready to use.

Sugar snap peas may be stir fried in a small amount of oil until crisp-tender. Boneless round steak provides an economical base for the following simple stir fried dish. I prefer to use a thick piece of family steak. If the meat is partially frozen, it is easy to cut into slices about ⅛ inch thick.

Stir-Fry Beef and Sugar Snap Peas

½ pound boneless round steak
2 teaspoons cornstarch
1 tablespoon dry sherry
2 tablespoons soy sauce
2 tablespoons oil
1 large onion, sliced
1 clove garlic, crushed
½ teaspoon finely-chopped fresh ginger
¼ cup broth, beef or chicken
2 cups stringed sugar snap peas

Partially freeze the steak and then cut it into ⅛ inch slices. Combine the cornstarch, sherry and soy sauce in a small bowl. Add the meat slices and stir to coat them well.

Heat the oil in a wok or large frying pan. Stir fry the steak, onion, garlic and ginger for about two minutes. Add the broth and the peas; cook for an additional two minutes. Serve over hot rice. Serves four.

I LIKE TO COOK outdoors on a charcoal grill, and one of my favorite meats to grill is a nice, thick piece of top round or family steak.

I cook the meat until it is medium rare and then slice it thinly across the grain. Since the meat is virtually fat free and boneless, a quarter of a pound of meat makes a generous serving.

Usually I just rub the meat with a little garlic salt, lemon pepper and Kitchen Bouquet before grilling it, but I also have a light marinade which gives the meat a slightly Oriental flavor.

The thinly-sliced meat can be served over a bed of rice and sprinkled with toasted sesame seeds, or delicious sandwiches can be made by stuffing the thinly-sliced meat, along with tomatoes and onions, into pocket breads.

This marinade can also be used with flank or sirloin steak.

Oriental Steak

½ cup soy sauce
¼ cup water
2 tablespoons lemon juice
1–2 cloves garlic, minced
2 tablespoons honey
2 green onions, including tops, chopped
¼ pound steak per serving

Combine the soy sauce, water, lemon juice, garlic, honey and onions. Add the steak and turn it to coat evenly. Marinate it in the refrigerator overnight or for at least several hours. Broil the meat to medium rare and cut across the grain into thin slices.

As THE WEATHER BEGINS to get cooler, menus at my house begin to change. I once again look at the oven as an important cooking tool and begin to think about putting the grill away.

When one of the stores had a special on boneless chuck roast last week, it inspired my first fall meal of the year. I marinated the roast in a spicy cider mixture and then put it in the oven to cook slowly. It filled my kitchen with a lovely aroma. About a half hour before serving time I added well-scrubbed new potatoes and green beans to the pan to make a one-dish meal.

The spices may be altered to suit what you have on hand, with a half teaspoon of ground spice being substituted for the tablespoon of each whole spice the recipe calls for. If you don't have little new potatoes, cut four large potatoes into quarters. Remember that the meat must be thoroughly dried or it won't brown nicely.

Autumn Pot Roast

3 pound boneless chuck roast
2 cups apple cider (approx.)
1 tablespoon peppercorns
1 tablespoon cloves
1 tablespoon celery seeds
1 tablespoon mustard seeds
1 tablespoon whole allspice
3 bay leaves
1 tablespoon oil
1 large onion, chopped
12 small new potatoes
½–1 pound green beans

Trim the meat of any excess fat, place it in a glass or ceramic bowl and add enough cider to completely cover it. Add the spices and the bay leaves. Marinate overnight in the refrigerator, turning the meat several times.

Lift the meat out of the marinade and scrape off all the seeds. Strain the marinade and set it aside. Heat the oil in a Dutch oven or large frying pan. Dry the meat thoroughly with a paper towel and then brown it well on both sides. Add the onion.

Pour enough of the marinade into the pot to make a depth of almost one inch. Cover and bake in a 350° oven for three hours or until the meat is tender. (The meat may also be simmered on top of the stove, if desired.) Check the liquid level occasionally, adding more marinade if needed. Then reduce any remaining marinade to ½ cup by boiling it uncovered in a small pan.

Scrub the potatoes thoroughly and cut the beans into inch lengths. Add the reduced marinade, potatoes and beans to the meat. Cover and cook until the vegetables are tender, about 15–20 minutes. Serves six.

Somehow pork seems more like a winter dish than something to serve during the summer. This probably was true when pork was a fatty meat, but today's hogs are lean and long. Pork chops are as excellent cooked over a charcoal fire as they are in the oven. Treat them just like a steak, cutting off any excess fat, making a few small cuts around the edges so that they won't curl, and salting and peppering to taste. Just remember, no rare ones please. It is necessary that pork be thoroughly cooked in order to eliminate the possibility of trichinosis. Grilled pork chops, potato salad, a vegetable, and applesauce make a pleasant summer meal.

I like to grill pork tenderloin occasionally. This would be good served with rice and sautéed sugar snap peas and water chestnuts.

Broiled Chinese-Style Pork Tenderloin

1 pork tenderloin, whole
1 tablespoon sherry
2 tablespoons soy sauce
2 tablespoons sugar
½ teaspoon cinnamon

Cut the pork tenderloin in half the long way. Mix the remaining ingredients together and rub into the meat; let this stand for one to two hours. Grill slowly until well done, turning frequently.

Slice the tenderloin into very thin diagonal slices. Serve with Chinese mustard, if desired; mix enough water or stale beer with the dry mustard to make a thin paste. Warning: the mustard will be very hot.

Orange Pork Chops

4 thick, lean pork chops
Salt and pepper to taste
2 tablespoons flour
1 or 2 oranges
½ cup orange juice

Arrange the chops in a shallow casserole. Sprinkle with salt, pepper and the flour. Peel and thinly slice the oranges and place the slices on top of the meat. Pour the orange juice over the top, cover and bake in a 350° oven for about 90 minutes or until the chops are tender. Serves four. Good with rice and a green salad.

BOTH APPETITES AND CULINARY inspiration are apt to wither when the temperature lingers in the nineties for several days. The other day I was trying to think of something to go with the green salad I had chilling in the refrigerator. I finally decided on a simple quiche, which tasted surprisingly good.

I know some people say quiche is a cliché, but the fact remains that they are easy to make (especially if you use a frozen pie crust), and they taste good. I think I like a basic cheese and bacon quiche best, although you may add a wide variety of ingredients. You can add seafood or various vegetables, from asparagus to zucchini (spinach is especially good), or you can use the basic cheese, egg, milk and cream mixture. Since many people feel quiche tastes best when it is lukewarm, it is even possible to bake the quiche in the cool of the morning and then serve it at room temperature or reheat it slightly at suppertime.

Quiche With Bacon

1 nine inch pie crust
¼ pound bacon, diced
1 cup (5 oz.) aged Swiss cheese, cubed
4 eggs
1 ½ cups either half-and-half or undiluted evaporated milk
1 teaspoon salt
¼ teaspoon white pepper
Pinch of nutmeg

Fry the bacon until it is crisp and drain it on a paper towel. Sprinkle the bacon and cheese over the bottom of the pie crust.

Beat the eggs only until they are well mixed. Stir into them the milk or cream, salt, pepper and nutmeg. Pour the egg mixture over the bacon and cheese.

Bake in a preheated 400° oven for 50–60 minutes. Remove from the oven and allow the quiche to cool at least 15 minutes before serving. Serves four to six.

I REALLY ENJOY GOING out for breakfast or brunch despite the fact that I am not really gung-ho about preparing breakfast for myself. Unfortunately, there aren't many places that serve elegant breakfasts in our area, so I am forced to remember breakfasts at the Commander's Palace in New Orleans and a little Swedish restaurant in Carmel, California.

I sometimes make menus for brunches which never seem to happen at my house. Every time a holiday weekend rolls around, I think wouldn't it be fun to do something different and have a brunch instead of a picnic or a buffet. But I never seem to get around to doing it.

But if I were to have a brunch this weekend, I would want to serve something that took advantage of the lovely fresh produce available at the Farmers' Market. I have a recipe that I brought back from California which would be perfect at this time of year. It reminds me of Eggs Benedict in execution but not in ingredients. It consists of a poached egg served on a slice of eggplant and topped with a fresh basil-scented tomato sauce.

If you do not have fresh basil available, you may substitute ½ teaspoon of crumbled dried basil. The ham may be easily left out of the sauce if you are cooking for vegetarians or prefer to avoid processed meats. This could also be served as a supper dish along with a fruit salad and some good crusty bread.

California Eggs Benedict

1 medium-sized eggplant
1 teaspoon salt
2 tablespoons butter or margarine
1 small onion, chopped
2 tomatoes
Salt and pepper to taste
1 teaspoon fresh basil, finely snipped
1 cup cooked ham, chopped
⅓ cup oil
6 eggs
Fresh basil leaves

Cut the unpeeled eggplant into six round slices. Sprinkle the salt over the slices to draw out some of the liquid and let stand about 30 minutes. Meanwhile, melt the butter in a skillet and sauté the onion until soft. Peel the tomatoes and gently squeeze out the seeds and any excess juice. Chop the tomato pulp and add it to the skillet. Also add the salt and pepper, snipped basil and cooked ham. Simmer for five minutes and then keep warm. Rinse and drain the eggplant and pat it as dry as possible with a paper towel. Heat the oil in a large skillet and fry the eggplant slices until they are browned and tender (5–8 minutes). Remove the eggplant from the skillet and drain on a paper towel; keep warm in a 175° oven.

In a small saucepan, poach the eggs. Place one poached egg on each slice of eggplant, top with the warm tomato mixture and garnish with fresh basil. Serve immediately. Serves six.

CHICKENS ARE MARVELOUS BIRDS. There must be more ways to prepare chicken for the table than any other meat. I can't think of a single ethnic cuisine which doesn't prepare chicken in a special way. Sometimes it is used as the basis of peasant dishes; in other cases its preparation is elevated to the level of haute cuisine.

Today chicken farming is a major industry. Millions of birds each year are shipped to market at approximately nine weeks of age. Old timers will comment that these birds don't have the flavor of chickens that were allowed to scratch for part of their diet. This is probably true, but a modern chicken can still provide the basis for a tasty meal if a little care is taken in the preparation.

Boneless, skinless chicken breasts can be used in a variety of ways to produce a quick and easy good-tasting main course. They are the raw material for chicken Kiev, brandied chicken breasts, many Oriental dishes, or just a simple sautéed breast which is hard to beat for flavor. A boneless chicken breast can also be used in place of expensive veal in many recipes. The most important thing to remember is not to overcook them. The meat should only be cooked until it is white throughout. This will probably take about ten minutes. If overcooked, the meat will become tough and dry.

Breaded Chicken Breasts

½ chicken breast per person
Flour
Salt and pepper to taste
1 egg (enough for four portions of chicken)
2 tablespoons water
1 cup (or more) bread crumbs
½ cup oil
1 tablespoon butter
Lemon slices for garnish

Place the skinless, boneless half breasts, one at a time, between two pieces of waxed paper or plastic wrap. Flatten slightly by pounding with the flat side of a cleaver or with the bottom of a pan. Dredge (cover the breasts on all sides) in the flour seasoned with salt and pepper.

Beat the egg with the water in a shallow dish. Dip the meat in the egg. Now dip the meat in the bread crumbs to coat. (An interesting variation can easily be made by adding ¼ cup grated Parmesan cheese to the crumbs.) Heat the oil and butter in a skillet and add the chicken pieces. Cook until golden brown on one side, about 3 to 5 minutes. Turn and cook about the same length of time on the other side. Remove and serve hot, garnished with lemon slices.

Buttered noodles sprinkled with poppy seeds and carrots browned in butter go well with this dish.

One of my favorite casseroles is duck cooked with pinto beans. It is nicely seasoned with onion, oregano and basil, and the flavor of the duck permeates the beans. It tastes very good.

The dish does have one drawback, however. It looks bland. The beans cook up to sort of a brownish gray, the duck is brown, the color is cooked out of the herbs, and the onion assumes the color of the beans. Any spaghetti casserole looks good in comparison.

Some people might ignore this lovely casserole except those who are willing to try a little bit of everything or people, like my husband, who practice a sort of reverse psychology. He has concluded that many things which appear unattractive have a great taste – oysters, for example.

You might enjoy this casserole at holiday time because like any dish made with dried beans, it is even better warmed up than it is fresh from the oven. Make it when you have time and heat it up when you need it. Serve the casserole with a colorful orange, onion, and lettuce salad or a deep green spinach salad, a hearty red wine, and some crusty French bread, and you will have a meal worthy of a party.

A hint for your budget: You can easily use duck with parts missing, which is on sale periodically. The parts which are missing are usually either wings or a portion of the drumstick. Since the duck is cut up before cooking in this recipe, the missing parts are not apparent.

The beans should be soaked in cold water overnight before they are cooked. Remember not to salt the beans until they are almost done so that they remain tender. Don't let the beans boil; they should be simmered gently so that they remain whole. If you wish, you may cook the beans at one time and finish the casserole at another time.

Duck With Pinto Beans

2 cups pinto beans
1 medium onion, stuck with 3 cloves
1 teaspoon oregano
1 tablespoon salt
¼ pound salt pork, diced
One 5–6 pound duck
Flour seasoned with salt and pepper
1 large onion, chopped
1 teaspoon dried basil
Pepper to taste

Put the presoaked, drained beans in a large saucepan with the oregano and the onion stuck with cloves. Cover with boiling water and simmer very gently until the beans are tender, 2½–3 hours. Add more water as necessary. Add the salt and simmer a few more minutes. Drain the beans, reserving the liquid.

Cook the salt pork in a large skillet until crisp and brown. Remove and reserve the crisp pieces.

Cut the duck into serving pieces, like a chicken. Coat the pieces with seasoned flour and brown them in the hot pork fat.

Mix together the beans, crisp pork, chopped onion and basil. Add pepper to taste. Put half of the beans in the bottom of a large casserole, arrange the duck pieces over the beans and cover with the remainder of the beans. Add the reserved bean liquid and enough boiling water to cover the beans. Cook in a 350° oven for 1½ hours, or until the duck is done. Add more liquid if necessary—the finished dish should be moist, but not wet.

When the casserole is done, remove the pieces of duck, take the meat off the bones, cut it into bite-sized pieces and stir it back into the beans. This distributes the meat evenly and makes the dish easier to serve and eat.

Here is a recipe using left-over turkey, which is a change of pace from a turkey sandwich or creamed turkey on biscuits. It uses left-over dressing to form the crust for a quiche rich with Swiss cheese and pieces of turkey that even a real man might enjoy!

Turkey Quiche

2 ½ to 3 cups left-over dressing
1 cup finely-chopped turkey
1 cup shredded Swiss cheese
4 eggs
One 5 ⅓ ounce can evaporated milk
⅛ teaspoon pepper

Press the dressing into the bottom and up the sides of a well-greased 9 inch pie plate. Bake for 10 minutes in a preheated 400° oven. Turn the oven temperature down to 350°. Mix together the turkey and cheese and sprinkle over the crust. Combine the eggs, evaporated milk and pepper in a small bowl; pour over the turkey and cheese. Bake in the 350° oven for 30–35 minutes or until the tip of a knife inserted in the center of the quiche comes out clean. Serves four to six.

We all know that good food is supposed to look good as well as taste good. Restaurants achieve this by carefully choosing the garnishes which will compliment each entree in color, taste and texture. Potatoes may be sculpted into tiny ovals while the zucchini is shredded before sautéing and the tomato appears as a rose. These little touches can also be achieved at home, but we quite often don't take the time for them. Luckily good fresh food that hasn't been over-cooked or left in the pan too long while the family assembles, usually looks and smells pretty good without adornment.

There are also some dishes which turn out very attractively because of the ingredients used. Here is a recipe for boneless chicken breasts cooked with dried apricots, which is simple to make and very attractive to serve. Serve with rice, a spinach salad, and cups of good jasmine tea and you will have a meal that you can be proud to put on the table.

Chicken With Apricots

2 pounds boneless skinned chicken breasts
16 dried apricot halves
1 tablespoon butter or margarine
1 ½ cups chopped onions
1 ½ teaspoon grated fresh ginger
Pinch of turmeric (optional)
1 inch piece cinnamon stick
Salt and pepper to taste
2 cloves garlic, minced
Juice of one lime
1 tablespoon honey
Pistachios or sliced almonds for garnish

Cut the chicken breasts into 1 ½ inch cubes. Cut the apricot halves in half. Sauté the onions and ginger in the butter until the onions soften. Add the turmeric, cinnamon stick, salt and pepper, and garlic and stir thoroughly. Add the chicken pieces and sauté until the chicken is just opaque. Lower heat, cover the pan and cook for ten minutes. Add the apricots and cook an additional 10 minutes. If the mixture seems very dry, up to ¼ cup stock or water may be added. Remove the chicken to a warm serving platter. Deglaze the pan with the lime juice and honey and pour over the chicken. Garnish with a sprinkling of pistachios or sliced almonds. Serves four to six.

I DON'T KNOW WHETHER to call this a recipe or not because I am not going to be very exact on either the ingredients or the method of preparation, but I hope it will provide inspiration for a meal that you will enjoy. The chicken or pork, served with white or wild rice, or a combination of both, and your favorite green salad would make a pleasant ending to a long winter day.

This is a way of preparing either pork chops or chicken pieces with dried apricots and seasoned with the proverbial pinch of cinnamon, nutmeg and/or ginger, as you choose, and either simmered on top of the stove or baked in the oven.

Chicken (Pork Chops) in Apricot Sauce

4 serving-sized pieces of chicken or 4 lean pork chops
Flour
1 tablespoon butter
1 tablespoon oil
Salt and pepper to taste
16–20 dried apricot halves
½ cup white wine, chicken broth or water
1 tablespoon brown sugar
Pinch of cinnamon, nutmeg and /or ginger
2–3 thinly-sliced green onions or 3–4 tablespoons
    toasted sliced almonds

Pat the meat dry with a paper towel and dredge the pieces in flour. Melt the butter and oil together in a large frying pan and brown the meat over high heat for 4–5 minutes per side. Add salt and pepper. Add the apricot halves and the ½ cup of liquid and sprinkle with brown sugar. Add the desired spices.

Bring to a boil, cover and simmer 20–25 minutes or until the meat is done, or cover and bake in a preheated 375° oven for 25 minutes. Top with green onions or almonds before serving on white or wild rice. Serves four.

Miscellaneous

When my husband's brother and his wife visited us last week, it was cool enough to cook a favorite family dinner for them: roast pork, gravy, dumplings, sauerkraut and applesauce. I grew up in a family where the roast was accompanied by mashed potatoes, but after twenty years of marriage, I'm almost convinced that dumplings belong with roast pork.

I have experimented with various types of dumplings with varying degrees of success. I have finally come up with a recipe which produces a firm, but fairly light dumpling. The toasted bread cubes help keep the dumplings from becoming soggy. If you form the dumpling on a piece of waxed paper, you can lower it into the water on the paper and then remove the paper as it becomes wet. In theory, you should be able to brown leftover dumpling slices in butter and serve with the leftover meat and gravy. I have never tried this, however, because I have never had any leftover dumplings.

Bohemian Roll Dumplings

2 beaten eggs
½ cup milk
2 cups flour
1½ teaspoons salt
2 teaspoons baking powder
2 slices white bread, toasted and cubed

Mix the eggs and milk together. Sift or stir together the flour, salt and baking powder and stir the mixture into the milk and eggs. Stir in toasted bread cubes. Divide the dough in half and shape into two rolls about five inches long on a piece of waxed paper. Let rest 30 minutes. Reshape if necessary and place them in a large Dutch oven or steamer containing three inches of simmering water. Cook covered for 15 minutes and then turn the dumplings over and cook them for 15 minutes on the other side. Remove to a platter and slice into one inch thick slices. Serves four to eight.

CHICKEN BROTH WITH DUMPLINGS is my family's favorite soup, especially with German dumplings called nockerln. You can start with canned chicken broth or you can make the broth from a package of unboned chicken breasts. I make the broth by putting the bones and skin in a large pan, adding a small onion, a stalk of celery, and a few pepper corns, covering with cold water and bringing to a boil. After I skim off the scum that rises to the top, I simmer the broth for a least an hour and a half. I remove the bones and skin, strain the broth through a fine sieve, and salt to taste. You will probably have a quart and a half of good broth.

Nockerln

(German Dumplings)

¼ cup soft butter or margarine
1 egg
1 cup flour
⅛ teaspoon salt
6 tablespoons milk

Beat the butter until it is creamy; add the egg and mix thoroughly. Stir in the flour and salt. Gradually add the milk until a firm batter is formed. Using a teaspoon, drop small balls of the batter directly into the boiling broth. Turn down the heat, cover the pan, and simmer for 10 minutes.

When you have a houseful of company, breakfast is sometimes a problem. It seems that you can never get the whole crew together to sit down at the same time.

One solution to this problem is setting up as a short-order cook and resigning yourself to spending the morning in the kitchen. Another solution is setting up a breakfast buffet and then going on about your own business. A bowlful of sliced, sweetened fresh fruit, an electric skillet of scrambled eggs, good bread, plenty of hot coffee, tea, orange juice, and cold milk should get everyone off to a good start.

The following scrambled eggs can be covered and held for up to two hours in a 200° oven or electric frying pan.

Patient Scrambled Eggs

½ cup butter
12 eggs
1 ⅓ cups milk
1 teaspoon salt
⅛ teaspoon pepper
2 tablespoons flour
2 tablespoons chopped chives (optional)

Melt the butter in a large skillet over low heat. Combine the remaining ingredients in a large bowl and beat with a rotary beater until smooth and well blended. Pour the eggs into the skillet and stir from the outside edge toward the center, allowing the uncooked egg in the center to flow to the outside. Continue stirring until all the egg has cooked and has a creamy appearance. Serves six to eight.

LEMONS ARE IN. Foods are in or out of fashion just the way clothes are, and judging by the number of food articles and new cookbooks featuring lemons, they are definitely in fashion.

There are many reasons for the popularity of lemons, with their fresh, zesty, piquant flavor leading the list. Nothing else tastes quite like a fresh lemon. For the diet conscious, lemons are high in Vitamin C, calcium and potassium, and low in calories and sodium. A few drops of lemon juice can serve as a substitute for a few shakes of the salt shaker.

I always remove the zest, or yellow portion of the skin, before squeezing a lemon. This can be done with a fine vegetable grater, a sharp potato peeler, or a handy little gadget called a zester. If I have no immediate use for the zest, I wrap it in a small piece of plastic wrap and stick it in the freezer until I want it. While it is easier to remove the zest while a lemon is cold, lemons give the maximum juice when they are warm. So if you have been storing your lemons in the refrigerator, run hot water over them for a couple of minutes before squeezing them.

The Vitamin C, or ascorbic acid, in lemon juice can act as a preservative for fresh fruits and vegetables. The use of lemon juice to prevent the discoloration of cut apples and peaches is well known. The lemon juice actually inhibits a chemical reaction which turns the fruit brown. A little lemon juice also keeps cauliflower white while it cooks and cuts down on the smell of the cooking vegetable too. You might want to try adding a few drops of lemon juice to cooking potatoes and rice for a fresher taste and brighter white.

A tablespoon or two of lemon juice can be added to almost any chicken or vegetable soup. You won't be able to taste the lemon flavor, but the soup will have a zip it didn't have before. A little melted butter, with the addition of lemon juice and perhaps a little of the zest, makes a perfect, simple sauce for fresh vegetables or fish. Lemon juice and dill weed added to plain yogurt also makes a fresh tasting sauce for fish, hot or cold, and for cold vegetables. For a lighter taste, use lemon juice in place of vinegar in your favorite salad dressing.

If you are marinating meat to grill, add a little lemon juice. The acid in the lemon will help tenderize the meat. A good marinade for steaks can be made with lemon juice, Dijon mustard, oil, dry sherry and soy sauce. Experiment to find your own special combination. Marinade the meat for an hour or so and then baste with the mixture as the steaks grill over hot coals.

Let's not forget about fresh lemonade, one of the best thirst quenching beverages there is. It is appropriate at picnics or at parties.

The Best Lemonade

1 ½ cups sugar, according to taste
1 cup water
1 ⅓ cups fresh lemon juice
Finely grated zest from 4 lemons
8 cups cold water
Ice cubes or crushed ice
Lemon slices for garnish (optional)

Combine the sugar and one cup of water in a small sauce pan over medium heat and bring to a boil. Reduce the heat and simmer about 5 minutes. Making this simple syrup insures that the sugar is completely dissolved, thereby avoiding sour first glasses and too-sweet later ones. Cool completely. Combine the sugar syrup, lemon juice and zest in a large pitcher. Add the cold water and stir vigorously. When ready to serve, put ice in tall glasses and fill them with lemonade. Garnish with a lemon slice if desired.

As SURE AS THE last rose of summer appears in the flower garden, the last zucchini will appear in the vegetable garden. Here is a recipe that combines the last of the season's zucchini with the apples of autumn.

Zucchini Applesauce

2 medium zucchini, peeled and diced
2 large tart apples, peeled, cored and diced
½ cup water
¼ cup sugar or to taste
½ teaspoon salt
2 whole cloves
1 tablespoon lemon juice
½ teaspoon cinnamon

Place the zucchini, apples, water, sugar, salt and cloves in a large saucepan and bring to a boil. Reduce the heat and simmer, covered, for 20 minutes, stirring occasionally. Remove the cover and continue cooking until all the liquid has evaporated. Discard the cloves and run the mixture through a food mill; mash or blend until it's smooth. Stir in the lemon juice and cinnamon. Serve either warm or cold. Makes 2 cups.

Granola has almost become a way of life for many Americans. It's eaten for breakfast, for snacks, with yogurt for lunch, as a topping for dessert, and as an ingredient in baked goods. Some granolas are mainly oatmeal while others are chock full of goodies like coconut, sunflower seeds and nuts. Some are very sweet and others have just a touch of honey for sweetening. There are whole sections of supermarket shelves devoted to granola cereals, but the best ones are those made at home.

Here is a health-food type granola recipe. I like it made with cashews, sunflower seeds and coconut.

Linda's Granola

1 cup wheat germ
8 cups of oatmeal
1 cup chopped nuts (cashews, walnuts, almonds or peanuts)
1 cup sesame or sunflower seeds (optional)
1 cup coconut (optional)
½ cup oil
½ cup honey
2 teaspoons vanilla

In a large, shallow roasting pan mix together the wheat germ, oatmeal, nuts, seeds and coconut. In a small pan, heat together the honey and oil until quite warm; add the vanilla. Pour over the dry ingredients and mix thoroughly.

Bake in a preheated 325° oven for 30 minutes, stirring every 10 minutes. Cool and pack in an air-tight container. Makes about 12 cups.

THE FLU THAT HAS been going around with all its aches, followed by an ear ache which has had me doctoring for more than a week, have combined to give me a rather jaundiced view of this holiday season.

The cookies and baked goods I had begun squirreling away in the freezer before Thanksgiving are for the most part still sitting there, the invitations are unwritten along with the Christmas cards, and the decorations are still in the big Christmas box.

Meals have also been left uncooked and nothing tastes good except those old comforting favorites, chicken soup and milk toast, a dish that my family says you have to be sick, really sick, to eat, let alone enjoy. They will join me, however, in having a cup of hot chocolate made with the extra hot milk.

Most times a cocoa mix from a jar will make a satisfying cup of cocoa, but there are times when only the taste of real chocolate will do, even if you just melt chocolate chips, the real chocolate ones, into a cup of hot milk and add sugar to taste.

Here are three recipes for hot chocolate drinks which I had been saving to share with you when the weather demanded a hot pick-me-up. The first is simple enough to serve to your family whenever they want a cup of cocoa. The last one is elegant enough to serve to company.

French Breakfast Chocolate

4 cups whole milk
3 ounces semi-sweet chocolate
1 teaspoon instant coffee (optional)
Sugar cubes

In a heavy saucepan warm the milk until it begins to steam. Add the chocolate and stir until blended in. Add the instant coffee if desired. Pour into mugs and serve immediately along with the sugar cubes, so each person can sweeten his or her cup as desired. Serves four to six.

Mexicans and Norwegians have their own special ways to make hot chocolate drinks. The Mexicans even have an intricately carved wooden tool that they use to whip their national chocolate drink into froth.

Mexican Chocolate

4 cups whole milk
6 ounces semi-sweet chocolate
⅓ cup slivered almonds
2 tablespoons sugar
3 cinnamon sticks, slit lengthwise

In a heavy saucepan, warm the milk until it begins to steam. Add the chocolate, almonds and sugar to a blender and whirl until the almonds are finely chopped. Add one half of the hot milk and whirl again. Add the remainder of the hot milk and whirl until the mixture is foamy. Place a piece of cinnamon stick in each cup and fill with the hot foamy chocolate. Serves six.

Norwegian Chocolate

½ cup whipping cream
2 tablespoons rum
6 cups whole milk
2 tablespoons sugar
2 tablespoons baking cocoa
2 tablespoons butter
Ground cinnamon

Whip the cream until it forms soft peaks and then beat in the rum; set aside. Heat the milk in a heavy saucepan. Mix together the sugar and the cocoa and add enough of the milk mixture to make a paste. Add the cocoa paste to the milk in the pan and heat it until it begins to steam, stirring occasionally. Whisk in the butter and serve from a teapot. Top each serving with the whipped cream and cinnamon. Serves six to eight.

SUMMER SCHEDULES AROUND OUR house are pretty flexible, changing as activities change. Sometimes one member of the family is up and out of the house hours before another member even begins to think about leaving the comforts of bed. This means that breakfast becomes an individual do-it-yourself project.

I make sure that there is milk, fruit or juice, cereal and bread available and then hope everyone eats a good breakfast, or at least eats some breakfast.

One thing I like to have on hand is homemade granola. It provides good stick-to-the-ribs nutrition without being laden with lots of extra sugar. It also is a good snack either eaten plain or mixed with yogurt.

Here is a recipe for a peanut butter flavored granola which is a little bit different in taste. I usually use cashews when I make granola, but if you really like the taste of peanuts, use them.

In fact, that is one of the nice things about homemade granola — you can load it with your own personal favorites. If you like the taste of sesame seeds, you can substitute them for all, or half, of the sunflower seeds. If you prefer dates to raisins, use them. Or leave the raisins out altogether if that pleases you.

Peanut Butter Granola

2 tablespoons vegetable oil
⅓ cup honey
⅓ cup peanut butter
1 teaspoon vanilla
3 cups rolled oats (oatmeal)
¼ cup wheat germ
½ cup sunflower seeds
½ cup chopped nuts
½ cup raisins

In a small saucepan, heat together the oil, honey, peanut butter and vanilla, stirring constantly until the mixture is smooth. Place the rolled oats, wheat germ, sunflower seeds and nuts in a large shallow pan; I use the broiler pan that came with my oven. Pour the peanut butter mixture over the dry ingredients and stir to mix thoroughly.

Bake the granola in a preheated 300° oven for 20–25 minutes, stirring every 5 minutes. Remove from the oven and cool completely before stirring in the raisins. Store in an airtight container. Makes about 5–6 cups of granola.

The Northfield Library

I LIKE LIBRARIES. And I think that Northfield has many reasons to be proud of the addition to the town's Carnegie Library, whose dedication will take place next week. The remodeling job is of such high quality that all can be proud of it even if they did not support the project whole-heartedly.

I can remember my first visit to the Northfield Public Library when I was a college student. I wanted a children's book for a class I was taking, so I strolled down the hill to see what I could find. As I walked in the door, I remember thinking, "How quaint!" At the time I had no idea that I would someday live in Northfield and that this was the first of many visits I would make to the building.

While I was serving on the library board, it became increasingly apparent that the adjective, quaint, had to be replaced by the word, inadequate. The building was not accessible to the handicapped. The staff was forced to work in the furnace room where books and magazines were also stored next to the antiquated heating system. The book collection was limited by the amount of shelving available. Patrons were beginning to ask for services and information in new forms, which the library could not even think of offering because there was literally no room for anything new.

After a good deal of controversy and a lot of hard work by many citizens and the library staff, the addition and remodeling have become a reality. No one will call the new library quaint. We are very lucky to be able to retain the graciousness that seemed to go with libraries when they were mainly a repository for books (and dreams), while also having access to new technologies.

It may be a shock to some that it will be possible to watch videocassettes, listen to music or use a computer at the library, that it will be possible to check out tapes or videocassettes as well as books, or that the friendly people behind the check-out desk use computers and microfiche as well as pencils and rubber stamps. However, the blending of the new and old architecture serves as a reminder that the library will also continue to serve its traditional uses. It looks like a library and smells like a library. It contains books to read and study and dream over, tables to work at, and a staff to help solve problems.

All this may seem a long way from recipes or things to eat unless you realize, as I do, what an important kitchen resource the library is. There are books that can help remodel a kitchen or show how to use garden produce. Cookbooks and magazines show what the rest of the world is eating and how to prepare the exotic right at home.

After a good grounding in the fundamentals of food preparation by my mother's side, books and magazines have taught me how to cook. Books taught me the basics of nutrition, illustrated new cooking techniques and presented the almost infinite possibilities of what can be done with food. Books have made possible the addition of my own versions of pasta primavera and chocolate mousse to the recipes for macaroni and cheese and chocolate pudding that came from my mother.

Perhaps just for today, I should change the heading on my column to "Reads Good!" and urge you to visit the library sometime soon.

Eating in Italy

To COMPLEMENT THE FLAVOR of northern Italy described in my columns on Natale Bread Salad and Zuppa Florentina, here are some highlights of the remainder of our month-long trip.

After leaving Florence, we moved on to Bologna. One of the main reasons for visiting Bologna is to eat. The arcaded streets provide pleasant strolling and there are museums and churches to visit, but the food is what attracted us. Bologna supposedly serves the best pasta in Italy and I believe that it's true. We ate delicious, fresh pasta usually sauced with some combination of cream, cheese, tomato, a bit of meat and one of the many types of mushrooms which are displayed in the restaurant windows. I enjoyed the wide variety of tastes, from slightly woodsy to the almost overpowering musky taste of truffles. I realized how much poorer our tables are, which know only the mild white variety of mushrooms normally available in the supermarket.

Gramigna, a small hollow pasta I had never seen before proved to be my favorite dish, baked with mushrooms, sausage, cheese and cream. The use of finely-diced fresh tomatoes both as a garnish and as an ingredient of various sauces and gravies is a Bolognese touch which could be adapted here now that good tomatoes are readily available. (Peel and seed the tomatoes before chopping.)

Next we went to Assisi. I now know what the phrase, "a city set on a hill," means. Assisi sits high above the surrounding Umbrian plain. It is an old Etruscan city, its site probably chosen because it was easy to defend. Now it is known as the home of St. Francis, that most peaceful of saints. We went there in order to visit a hill town and to see the art in the large double Basilica of San Francesco. We stayed at a guest house run by the Franciscan Sisters of Atonement, an order of teaching nuns from upper New York State. They maintain a guest house in Assisi that was a lovely place to stay. We had a room with a balcony overlooking the gardens and roofs of the town.

While in Assisi, we ate in the most beautiful spot in which I have ever eaten. Most of the time I am more interested in what is on the plate than what surrounds the plate, but the tree-covered terrace of the Hotel Subasio was beautiful. We sat near a fountain overlooking the green and gold Umbrian countryside with the cathedral walls forming a backdrop for the swooping swallows. Perhaps almost anything would have tasted good there.

Pancakes

St Olaf - Ytterboe Hall   P Lampe

Fresh raspberries are now available at the Farmers' Market and at places in the country where you can pick your own. They are a special treat not available in many places because the berries do not pack or ship well. Fresh berries go especially well with this pancake recipe, a tradition in my family.

P.D. Eastman has written a delightful children's book titled, "Are You My Mother?" It is about a mother bird who goes off to find something for her baby to eat when she realizes that her egg is about to hatch. The egg hatches before she returns and the baby bird sets off to find his mother. He asks each animal and machine he meets, "Are you my mother?" At the end of the book he finds his very own mother with the food she has found for him. These pancakes are the all time favorite of my own "baby birds." Our oldest son even had one shellacked which hangs on his college dormitory wall! This is a Swedish recipe, but at our house the cakes are always called Baby Bird Pancakes.

Baby Bird Pancakes

(Swedish Sour Cream Pancakes)

4 eggs, separated
1 cup flour
1 cup milk
1 teaspoon sugar
½ teaspoon salt
4 tablespoons (¼ cup) sour cream

Beat the egg whites until stiff. In another large bowl, beat the egg yolks until light and lemon colored. Then add the flour, sugar, salt and milk and beat until smooth. Stir in the sour cream and then fold in the egg whites. Bake by rounded tablespoonfuls on a hot buttered griddle or in a large skillet. Makes 4 to 5 dozen small pancakes. Serve with sweetened fresh fruit, lingonberries or applesauce, and powdered sugar.

Last week I had a group of good friends in for lunch. I wanted to serve something which would taste good, be appropriate to the changing season, and be fairly quick to make, since I would not be home the hour or so before noon.

I settled on serving apple pancakes with cinnamon sugar, sausage and lots of good coffee—not a typical "ladies luncheon" menu but one which met with the approval of my guests.

If you have a food processor, you could put it to good use in cutting the apples into julienne strips. If you don't have a food processor, you can slice the apples very thin with a knife or grate them coarsely. As long as the apple pieces are thin enough so that they cook quickly, it really doesn't make too much difference what shape they are.

Before I left the house, I stirred up the batter, peeled the apples, quartered them, and put the quarters in a bowl of water to which I had added a couple of tablespoons of lemon juice. When I got home, I grated the apples, stirred them into the batter and had lunch ready by the time my guests arrived.

Apple Pancakes

1 cup flour
½ teaspoon salt
3 teaspoons sugar
1 ½ cups cold milk
4 eggs
3 to 4 large, tart apples

Place the flour, sugar and salt in a mixing bowl. Stir in the milk to make a smooth paste. Add the eggs one at a time beating briskly after each addition. Peel and core the apples and either cut into fine julienne strips, grate coarsely, or slice thinly. Stir the apple pieces into the batter and fry small-sized cakes (¼ cup batter) in butter on a griddle. Serve with cinnamon sugar. Serves four.

We lived for several years in Holland, Michigan, where we became familiar with tulip festivals, wooden shoes, windmills, Dutch cheeses and many delicious baked goods. When Prince Bernhard of the Netherlands came to give a convocation address at Hope College, he remarked that it was nice that Dutch traditions were being preserved somewhere. Pannekoeken, oven-baked, popover-like pancakes, are a popular ending to a Dutch meal. They may be served with traditional toppings such as black cherry preserves with thin slivers of fresh ginger or cooked apple slices, which are topped with a cinnamon-sugar mixture. They are also good just buttered and sprinkled with powdered sugar and a little lemon juice. Any lightly sweetened sliced fresh fruit also makes an excellent topping.

In a non-traditional way, a pannekoek makes an excellent base for any creamed mixture: chicken, shrimp, hard cooked eggs, mushrooms, to name just a few possibilities. If you wanted to add further Dutch accent to the dish, it could be topped with some grated Gouda cheese and popped under the broiler for a couple of minutes before serving.

Pannekoek

(Dutch Pancake)

2 eggs
½ cup flour
½ cup milk or light cream
¼ teaspoon salt
1 tablespoon butter

Preheat the oven to 450° and place a 9 inch ovenproof skillet on the lowest shelf to heat. Mix the eggs, flour, milk and salt together in a small bowl and beat until smooth. (Or place ingredients in a blender container and blend until smooth.) Remove the skillet from the oven and add the butter, rotating the pan so the butter melts and coats the pan. Add the batter immediately. Bake on the lowest oven shelf for 10 minutes; reduce heat to 350° and bake 10 minutes more. Serves two.

For dessert, cover with your favorite fruit, jam or preserves. Or butter and sprinkle with powdered sugar and lemon juice.

A German pancake or pfannkuchen makes a delicious light supper for two or dessert for four. If it looks like a lot for two people to eat, remember it is mostly hot air! We often had this when we lived in Germany with a sauce of sweetened cooked dried apricots, but it's good served with any sliced fresh fruit or even with just a dusting of powdered sugar and a squeeze of lemon juice.

Pfannkuchen

(German Pancake)

4 eggs, separated
2 tablespoons cornstarch
1/4 cup milk
1/4 cup warm water
1 tablespoon sugar
3/4 teaspoon salt
Grated rind of one lemon
2 tablespoons butter or margarine

Combine the beaten egg yolks, cornstarch, milk, water, sugar, salt and lemon rind and stir until smooth. Whip the egg whites until stiff and fold into the yolk mixture. Heat two tablespoons of butter in a 10 inch skillet until it just begins to brown. Put the batter in the pan and place in a pre-heated 400° oven until puffed and brown — 8 to 10 minutes. Serve at once. Good with a topping of sweetened fresh fruit, jam, or just powdered sugar and a squeeze of lemon juice.

The ratio of four eggs, two cups of milk and two cups of flour has lots of culinary possibilities. It can become crepes, popovers, or even Yorkshire pudding.

Crepes

2 cups flour
¼ teaspoon salt
4 eggs
2 tablespoons melted butter
2 to 2 ¼ cups milk

Sift or stir together the flour and salt. Add the eggs one at a time, mixing well with an electric mixer at low speed. Add the melted butter. Gradually stir in the milk while mixing constantly. The batter should be the consistency of thin cream. If it seems too thick, add a little more milk.

Let the batter rest an hour or two before cooking the crepes in a well-buttered 6 inch frying pan over medium high heat. Keep the crepes warm in a 250° oven until all are cooked. The recipe makes about 16 crepes. For a main dish, fill them with your favorite creamed meat, seafood or vegetable mixture, or for dessert, with a favorite jam.

No-Beat Popovers

2 eggs
1 cup milk
1 cup flour
½ teaspoon salt

Break the eggs into a bowl and add the milk, flour and salt. Mix well with a spoon, disregarding lumps. Fill well-greased custard cups or deep muffin pans three-quarters full. Place them in a cold oven, set the thermostat for 450°, turn on the heat and bake for 30 minutes without peeking. Makes nine to ten popovers.

I AM ALWAYS ON the lookout for different pancake recipes, and lately I have also been thinking about the care and feeding of children who have become vegetarians. These two concerns led me to a basic cottage cheese pancake, which can be fortified with wheat germ, finely-chopped dried fruit, sunflower seeds, chopped nuts, grated apple or a combination of any of these. Wheat germ, sunflower seeds and apples taste good together.

If the pancakes are stirred up in a blender or food processor, the batter will be practically lump free; otherwise, the lumps caused by the cottage cheese particles will persist, but the pancakes will still be good.

Nutritious Cottage Cheese Pancakes

1 ½ cups (12 ounces) cottage cheese
6 eggs
1 tablespoon sugar
½ teaspoon cinnamon (optional)
¼ teaspoon nutmeg (optional)
½ cup unbleached flour
Pinch of salt
Butter or margarine for frying
Optional Additions:
2 tablespoons wheat germ
8 finely-chopped dried apricots
¼ cup sunflower seeds
¼ cup chopped nuts
1 large tart apple, peeled, cored and finely grated

Add the cottage cheese, eggs, sugar, cinnamon, nutmeg, flour, salt and any optional ingredients to the container of a blender or the work bowl of a food processor and process for about 30 seconds; scrape down the sides of the container and whirl again for about 10 seconds. (Or place the ingredients in a large bowl and beat for two minutes; scrape the sides and bottom of the bowl and beat for an additional minute.)

Spoon the batter onto a hot buttered skillet or griddle to form pancakes about 2 ½ inches in diameter. Cook until golden brown on one side and then turn and brown the other side. Make additional pancakes with the remaining batter, buttering the skillet as necessary. Serve with your favorite topping. Serves three.

Suggested toppings: Sliced and sweetened fresh fruit, cinnamon sugar, powdered sugar with or without a squeeze of fresh lemon juice, fruit or maple syrup, and fruit yogurt.

Here are two pancake recipes that are based on sour cream. The first is for an egg-rich, delicate pancake, which might fit into your breakfast or brunch plans on a holiday weekend. These pancakes would be good served with sausage and topped with a fruit sauce, which can easily be made by sweetening and thickening frozen fruit or by using canned fruit pie filling. Or you might like them topped with warm maple syrup and toasted chopped nuts.

Sour Cream Pancakes

4 eggs
1 cup sour cream
½ cup flour
¼ teaspoon salt
1 tablespoon sugar
¼ teaspoon baking soda

In a large bowl, beat the eggs well. Stir in the sour cream. Sift or stir together the flour, salt, sugar and baking soda and then stir it into the egg mixture. Bake small pancakes on a well-buttered, hot griddle. Turn the cakes over when holes appear around the edges. Top as desired. Serves two to four.

Feather cakes feature both cottage cheese and sour cream. These pancakes are good served with powdered sugar and an orange or lemon wedge to squeeze over the top. Or you might try substituting these pancakes for a traditional shortcake and serving them topped with crushed fresh strawberries. This recipe will make enough pancakes to serve three or four people for a main course or eight for dessert.

Feather Cakes

1 cup cottage cheese
1 cup sour cream
6 eggs
1 cup flour
1 tablespoon sugar
1 teaspoon baking powder

Put the cottage cheese in a blender and blend until it is smooth. Add the remaining ingredients and blend until thoroughly mixed, stopping the blender and scraping down the sides if necessary. Drop the batter by the tablespoonful on a hot (350°) buttered griddle. Cook until small holes appear in the top of the cakes; then turn them over and cook until the other side is brown. Keep the pancakes warm in a 250° oven until all the batter is baked. Serve topped with powdered sugar or your favorite sweetened fresh fruit.

THE CRITERIA I USE for selecting these recipes are first of all that the results taste good to me. This means that my personal food prejudices prevail for the most part. The second governing principle is that the recipes are fairly easy to prepare by someone who hasn't spent a lot of time in the kitchen.

I try to avoid recipes which call for special equipment or ingredients which aren't easily available in Northfield. I also try to follow a seasonal calendar.

Keeping with these principles, here is a vegetable pancake recipe. It is a fairly easy way to serve a combination of a vegetable and a starch at a main meal when combined with something like grilled chicken. The pancakes may also be eaten joyfully as the main course at breakfast or lunch.

Even children who usually turn up their noses at vegetables will often gladly eat these pancakes when topped with a little applesauce or a dab of syrup. I like these corncakes made with fresh corn, but canned corn may be used.

Corn Pancakes

1 cup flour
1 tablespoon sugar
2 teaspoons baking powder
½ teaspoon salt
1 egg
¾ cup milk
1 tablespoon oil
1 ½ cup corn (approximately)

In a medium-sized bowl stir together the flour, sugar, baking powder and salt. In another bowl whisk together the egg, milk and oil; stir in the corn. Add the wet ingredients to the dry ingredients and stir to blend.

Use about ¼ cup of batter for each pancake. Cook over moderate heat on a lightly greased griddle until the bottoms are golden brown and the tops have begun to bubble. Then flip the pancakes and cook them until their bottoms are nicely browned. Makes ten medium-sized pancakes.

Waffles always sound like a good idea for breakfast at our house to everyone except me. They usually involve separating eggs and, for some reason, I prefer not to deal with uncooked eggs before I have had my breakfast. This means that waffles appear for lunch or supper but not for breakfast.

However, I recently found a waffle recipe, which uses yeast as the leavening agent, and which can be stirred up the evening before you wish to serve them, then refrigerated overnight. In fact, the batter can be refrigerated for up to four days before baking. Now waffles can even be found on our breakfast table. For variety, chopped pecans, diced dried fruit, blueberries, crumbled crisp bacon or even chocolate chips can be sprinkled over the batter just before baking it.

If you are looking for a different sweet topping for waffles or pancakes, you might try mixing together one cup of sugar, one cup of heavy cream and one cup of maple syrup, bringing the mixture to a boil over medium heat. The topping should be served hot.

Leftovers should be refrigerated and reheated before serving.

Overnight Refrigerator Waffles

2 ½ cups warm water (110°)
1 package active dry yeast
1 teaspoon sugar
⅔ cup low-fat dry milk
⅓ cup oil
½ teaspoon baking soda
½ teaspoon salt
2 eggs
3 cups flour

In a large bowl combine the water, yeast and sugar and let stand five minutes to activate the yeast. Add the dry milk, oil, baking soda, salt, eggs and flour and beat until smooth. Cover and chill overnight.

Bake on a preheated waffle iron following the manufacturer's instructions. Cook until well browned. Makes seven or eight waffles using ¾ cup of batter for each waffle.

I LOVE TO GO into the garage these days because the apples I have stored there smell so good. It is such fun to drive out to an apple orchard and be able to choose from all the varieties of apples that grow in Minnesota. I prefer a tart, crisp apple, with Minjons being the sentimental favorite at our house for both eating and cooking. My children distinguish between home-made applesauce and commercial applesauce by the color, since Minjons produce such a pretty pink sauce.

When you have made applesauce, apple pie, and apple crisp and are looking for another apple recipe, you might want to try this recipe for a baked apple-cinnamon pancake. This family-sized pancake could be cut into six wedges and served as dessert, but I prefer to serve it with sausage as a main course for two or three.

Apple Pannekoek

6 tablespoons butter or margarine
2 teaspoons cinnamon
Scant ¼ cup sugar
2 large tart apples, peeled, cored, and thinly sliced
4 eggs
1 cup flour
1 cup milk
Powdered sugar

In a heavy 10 or 12 inch frying pan with an ovenproof handle, melt the butter over medium-high heat. Stir in the cinnamon and sugar. Add the apple slices and cook, while stirring, until the apples are translucent (about 5 minutes). Place the pan in a preheated 425° oven while you mix the batter.

In a blender or food processor, whirl the eggs and flour until smooth. Blend in the milk. Or you may just whisk the eggs, stir in the flour and then add the milk. Pour the batter evenly over the apples and return the pan to the oven. Bake uncovered until the pancake is puffy and golden (about 15 minutes). Dust with powdered sugar. Cut into wedges and serve immediately. Serves two to six.

Pasta

Carleton - Goodsell Observatory   P Lampe

When Americans think of Italian food, the combination of spaghetti and tomato sauce often comes to mind. In fact, more spaghetti and tomato sauce is probably served in this country than in Italy.

The Italians are much more broadminded when it comes to dressing their beloved pasta. They make many lovely sauces based on cream and cheese and add all sorts of fresh vegetables to their pasta dishes.

Here is a recipe for a version of the classic Italian dish, Pasta Primavera. I hope it will serve as a basis for your own creation. Remember that quantities and types given for the vegetables are not absolutes. Substitute what you have on hand and what you prefer. If you don't like carrots, try broccoli; if you don't want zucchini, use more peas. Try adding one cup of shrimp instead of the ham. Look at the recipe as a suggestion rather than a formula.

Homemade pasta will always be better than that bought at the store; but if you are not "into" homemade pasta, remember not to overcook whatever brand you use. If possible, use freshly-grated Parmesan cheese; it does make a difference, and Parmesan is usually available at a delicatessen counter.

Pasta Primavera

½ cup butter
1 large garlic clove, minced
1 medium onion, minced
1 pound asparagus, trimmed and diagonally cut into
  ¼ inch slices, tips left whole
8 ounces mushrooms, sliced
1 carrot, thinly sliced
1 medium zucchini, cut into ¼ inch slices
1 cup whipping cream
½ cup chicken broth
2 tablespoons fresh basil or 2 teaspoons dried
1 cup peas, fresh or frozen
2 ounces prosciutto or ham, minced
5 green onions, chopped
Salt and pepper
1 pound linguine, cooked al dente
1 cup freshly-grated Parmesan cheese

Heat a wok or large skillet over medium-high heat. Add the butter, garlic and onion and sauté them about two minutes. Add the asparagus, mushrooms, zucchini, and carrot and cook an additional 2 minutes. Remove several asparagus tips, mushroom slices and zucchini pieces and reserve them for a garnish.

Increase heat to high. Add the cream, broth and basil and boil about three minutes. Stir in the peas, ham and green onions and cook one minute more. Season to taste with salt and pepper.

Add the cooked pasta and the cheese, tossing until thoroughly combined. Turn onto a large serving platter and garnish with the reserved vegetables. Serve immediately. Serves four to six.

Here are two of my favorite pasta dishes. The first one is meatless. Alfredo sauce is usually served over noodles or linguini but for a change you might want to serve it over spinach noodles. Remember not to overcook the pasta that you use. It should be cooked al dente, so that it gives some resistance to the tooth when you bite into a strand.

Noodles Alfredo

A large pot of salted water
2 cloves garlic, very finely chopped
1 cup whipping cream
½ cup freshly grated Parmesan cheese
½ cup grated Provolone cheese
1 teaspoon basil
½ teaspoon salt
White pepper to taste
½ cup sour cream
8 ounces noodles

Place water on the stove to boil. In a large skillet sauté the garlic in butter for about one minute; the garlic should not brown. Add the whipping cream and bring to a boil. Reduce the heat and add the cheeses, stirring constantly until the cheese melts and the mixture thickens. Remove from the heat and add the basil, salt and pepper, and sour cream.

Cook the noodles according to the package directions (8–10 minutes) and drain. Reheat the sauce, but do not boil it. Arrange the noodles on a serving dish or platter and pour the hot sauce over them. Serve with additional grated Parmesan cheese, if desired. Serves four as a main dish or eight as a side dish.

Bowties (Farfalle) with Spinach, Bacon and Mushrooms

A large pot of salted water
½ pound thick-sliced bacon, cut into 1 inch squares
¼ cup butter or margarine
1 cup thinly-sliced green onions
½ cup diced sweet red pepper (optional)
1 cup chicken broth
2 tablespoons lemon juice
Salt
½ teaspoon pepper
1 package (1 pound) bowties (farfalle)
4 cups fresh spinach, washed and torn into bite-sized pieces (10 ounces)
½ pound fresh mushrooms, sliced
1 cup grated Parmesan cheese

Put the water on to boil. Cook the bacon in a large skillet until it is crisp. Drain the bacon on a paper towel and reserve it. Discard all but about two tablespoons of the bacon fat.

Add the butter to the two tablespoons of bacon fat and sauté the onions and pepper until tender, about 2 minutes. Add the chicken broth and lemon juice and bring to a boil. Simmer for about 2 minutes. Taste and add salt, if needed, and pepper. Set aside this sauce.

Cook and drain the bowtie pasta according to the label directions and return it to the pot. Add the mushrooms and spinach, tossing to mix. Add the sauce and toss over medium heat until the sauce is absorbed and the spinach wilted. Divide among four heated plates, top with Parmesan cheese and the reserved bacon. Serves four.

THE FARMERS' MARKET IS a joy to visit, with produce beautiful to behold. The eggplant has been spectacular recently. Not only are there the familiar plump purple ones, but there are also small white ones—which might be the variety responsible for the vegetable's English name—and long, slender, light-purple Japanese eggplant, which are so tender and sweet that they do not need peeling or salting (to remove bitter juices) before cooking. And the zucchini! There are little tiny ones still wearing their blossoms on one end and giant ones for stuffing and baking or grating to use in baked goods or casseroles.

There have also been some unusual offerings lately. One stand has had dried morels for sale. They are sold on an individual basis so you could buy just one and see if you like the rich, wild-mushroom taste. Try adding one (soaked for a few minutes in warm water and then cut into small pieces) to the pan when you are sautéing chops, or add one to your favorite steak or spaghetti sauce. The flavor also goes well with chicken.

There were some lovely blackberries, the modest price of which was hardly compensation for braving the plants' inch-long thorns! Fresh herbs—basil, parsley, dill and oregano—are also for sale. It should be about time for shallots to begin making their appearance. You can also buy honey, jams and jellies and a variety of fresh baked goods. And last but not least, there are beautiful flowers.

Here is the recipe for a mushroom and zucchini pasta topping, which is quick and easy to make. You might even be able to sneak the zucchini past the kids this way.

You can add about a pound of freshly-boiled shrimp and a half cup of whipping cream to this and have a very elegant and delicious one-dish meal.

Mushroom and Zucchini With Pasta

2 cloves garlic, minced
2 tablespoons butter
1 pound mushrooms, cleaned, trimmed and sliced
2 tablespoons lemon juice
4 small (one pound) zucchini, cut into matchstick-sized pieces
¼ cup parsley, minced
2 teaspoons dried basil
Salt and pepper to taste
2 tablespoons butter
1 pound hot, cooked pasta
Parsley for garnish

In a large heavy skillet over low heat, sauté one clove of garlic in two tablespoons of butter for a minute. Add the mushrooms and lemon juice and toss to mix thoroughly. Add the zucchini and increase the heat to medium high. Add salt and pepper, basil and parsley. Cover and cook for about three minutes, so that the zucchini is still crisp. Put the additional two tablespoons of butter and remaining clove of minced garlic into a large serving bowl. Add the hot, drained pasta and toss to mix. Add the vegetable mixture and toss again. Garnish with parsley if desired. Serves six to eight.

This classic Italian recipe is not a health food recipe, but it contains lots of healthful ingredients and it tastes good. If you can't find penne at the grocery store, any short tubular macaroni such as mostaccioli or even plain macaroni will do. If you use fresh spinach, be sure to wash it thoroughly in several sinks filled with cold water in order to remove all sand and grit.

Penne con Spinaci e Ricotta

(Pasta with Spinach and Ricotta)

One pound fresh, washed spinach, stems and roots removed, or one 10 ounce package of frozen leaf spinach, thawed
4 tablespoons butter or margarine
Salt
8 ounces (½ package) penne or other short tubular macaroni
½ cup ricotta cheese
⅓ cup freshly grated Parmesan cheese

If using fresh spinach, cook it in a covered pan over medium heat, with a pinch of salt and no more water than is clinging to the leaves. The leaves should be tender in less than 10 minutes. Cool the spinach.

Take the freshly cooked spinach or thawed frozen spinach and drain it well, squeezing out as much liquid as possible without squeezing the spinach into a solid ball. Finely chop or cut the spinach and set aside.

In a large saucepan or skillet, melt half of the butter over medium heat and sauté the spinach for 2 or 3 minutes. Salt the spinach liberally (this is all the salt that will be in the finished dish) and set aside.

Cook the pasta according to the directions on the package and drain well. Transfer the pasta to a warm serving bowl and reheat the spinach if necessary. Add the remaining butter, ricotta cheese, grated Parmesan cheese and the spinach to the pasta. Mix thoroughly and serve at once. Serves four to six.

Zucchini is a relative newcomer to the American table. The first seeds came from Italy in the 1920s and became available to the public in the 1933 Burpee seed catalog. American cooks soon discovered zucchini's versatility. It is able to carry the flavors of any dish in which it is incorporated and yet has its own subtle texture and taste. Zucchini now appears in the supermarket all year round, but the best is still grown in your own garden or bought at the Farmers' Market while it is at the height of its freshness.

This fast zucchini pasta entree is one that you can have ready for the table in the length of time it takes to cook the linguini or thin spaghetti. Since the oil plays an important role in the sauce, use the best olive oil you can find. The recipe calls for eight cloves of garlic, which may sound like a lot to a Midwesterner, but be adventuresome and try it. The timid can cut down on the garlic a little, but leaving it out altogether will produce a bland dish.

Linguini with Oil, Garlic and Zucchini

1 pound linguini, broken in half
¼ cup olive oil
8 cloves garlic, minced
3 medium zucchini, quartered lengthwise and sliced
¼ cup chopped fresh parsley
¼ cup olive oil
2 teaspoons dried oregano
Salt and pepper to taste
⅔ cup grated Parmesan cheese

Begin by cooking the linguini according to the directions on the package. Heat ¼ cup of olive oil in a large skillet. When it is hot, add the garlic and sauté over low heat for about 2 minutes, stirring frequently. Add the zucchini and cook until it is barely tender. Add the parsley and cook until the parsley is wilted and the zucchini is tender. The zucchini and linguini should be done at about the same time.

Drain the linguini and place it in a large, deep serving bowl. Add the remaining ¼ cup of olive oil, the zucchini mixture, oregano, salt and pepper and toss well. Add the Parmesan cheese and toss again. Serve immediately. Serves six generously.

"Tastes good!" was suddenly precipitated into the computer age at 9:15 AM, Thursday, Dec. 27, 1984, when I found myself without a typewriter.

Before I could go down to the basement and resurrect my good old Royal portable, which I had received as a high school graduation present more years ago than I really care to count, my husband asked, "Why don't you use the word processor?" He found my answer that all I wanted to do was type out my column unacceptable and immediately formatted a disc for me and sat me down in front of a screen on which glowing green letters appeared when keys were struck. Some of the letters mysteriously appeared in italics while others refused to appear at all, just because I pushed the key that is where the shift is on my old typewriter. 1984, here I am, better late than never.

Now back to the kitchen where I am more at home. Here is a recipe for a simple tomato cream pasta sauce. Lately I have been using quite a lot of pasta as the carbohydrate component of our dinners. This is partly because really good imported Italian pasta is now easily available at the grocery store and because competition from Italy has led to an improvement in American brands as well. A simple pasta dish, grilled chicken or even hamburger, and a salad provide a nice change-of-pace meal.

The tomato component of this sauce may be simmered ahead of time and refrigerated until needed, then reheated and the cream added just before serving. The tomato base could even be divided and used for two meals if your family is small.

Tomato Cream Pasta Sauce

¼ pound butter or margarine
3 tablespoons chopped onions
3 tablespoons chopped carrots
3 tablespoons chopped celery
2 ½ cups canned Italian tomatoes with juice
Salt to taste
½ teaspoon sugar
½ cup heavy cream

In a heavy saucepan, melt the butter, add the onions, celery and carrots, and sauté until the vegetables are slightly wilted. Add the tomatoes and simmer for about an hour, stirring occasionally. Add salt to taste and then the sugar. The sauce may be refrigerated or frozen at this point if it is not going to be used immediately.

Reheat and add the cream. Heat over medium heat for about a minute, stirring continually. The recipe makes enough sauce for one pound of cooked pasta.

On Easter we went to Sunday brunch in Minneapolis. Putting aside pictures of drought-wrecked northern Africa and inner-city Central America, we escaped for a little while into Thorstein Veblen's world of conspicuous consumption. The food was bounteous and beautifully arranged and, most important of all to me, it tasted good. It was marvelous to sit back with Jerry and good friends in a pleasant, sunlit room, filled with happy people and good music, and share food and wine and ideas and memories.

One of the hot dishes on the buffet table was a pasta dish made with curly noodles that Italians call tortiglioni; American manufacturers sometimes tag them with the funny name scoodles. The advantage of this type of pasta is that it holds lots of sauce; if you look carefully at the surface of imported, uncooked pasta, you will see that it is often scored with minute ridges for the same reason.

I initially passed by the dish because it looked like something I quite often make, but when my friend Lee said how good it was, I tried some. It was very similar to what I make, a simple adaptation of Noodles Alfredo or pasta primavera, depending on what is added to the basic noodle, with a simple sauce made of butter, cream and imported Parmesan cheese.

The thing to remember when making such a dish at home is that the quality of the finished product will depend on what you start with. If you use whole wheat pasta instead of an imported hard wheat variety, the texture of your dish will be different. If you use pre-grated Parmesan cheese instead of grating your own from a piece of Italian Parmesan, the taste will be very different. If you use milk instead of cream, the sauce will not be as smooth and rich.

In this dish, as in much cooking, you can make compromises in the ingredients, but then you must also expect the results to be different. The dish may really taste good, but it will not be what the original recipe produces. One of the fun things about cooking is that recipes can be altered to suit your own taste or nutritional concerns or even what is available in the kitchen or the local supermarket.

The quantities given in this recipe are for two servings; multiply or divide as you will. It is a very forgiving recipe; using approximate quantities will probably work well.

Pasta For Lee

6 ounces favorite pasta, uncooked
1 tablespoon butter
¼ cup heavy cream
5 tablespoons (or more) grated Parmesan cheese
Pepper to taste

Optional:
Minced garlic
Diced ham
Sliced zucchini
Shrimp
Cooked peas
Sautéed mushrooms
Your imagination

Cook the pasta in a large pan of boiling salted water until it is done to the consistency you prefer. Drain the pasta and return it to the pan. Quickly stir in the butter and then the cream. Toss with the Parmesan cheese. Taste for seasoning and add any optional ingredients you desire, which have been pre-warmed in a bit of butter. Serve immediately. Serves two.

ATTITUDE MAKES A CERTAIN amount of difference in the kitchen as it does elsewhere in life. Last week I made a very good cheese sauce to serve over some fresh asparagus. I used up all the odd bits and pieces of cheese that were languishing in my refrigerator, including one piece which I was unable to identify as to type or even place or time of origin. There were five different kinds of cheese in the sauce.

Now here is where attitude comes in. When I was asked about the sauce, I said, "Oh, I just cleaned out the refrigerator and used what was there." This left me with a very good tasting cheese sauce, but what I could have said was that I had made a sauce with five cheeses and fresh garden herbs. Then I would have been able to serve forth a gourmet treat. It would have been the same sauce and really tasted the same, but it certainly sounds more impressive and at a restaurant would have cost more. Perhaps when the kitchen blahs set in, all we really need is a more creative vocabulary and a change of attitude about what we are doing.

Here is a pasta-cheese recipe I have been working on, trying to duplicate a pasta dish I recently ate in Phoenix. It was so good that I was tempted to order an encore for dessert. The sauce is made by melting the cheese in cream at the very last moment before serving. I remove the spaghetti pot from the burner and put the skillet containing the sauce in its place, drain the pasta, and then stir the sauce a couple of times to make sure the cheeses are all melted and the sauce is smooth. Then I add the pasta to the sauce and toss gently to coat the pasta, while tasting for salt and pepper. I serve it immediately, before the pasta has a chance to absorb all the sauce.

The exact measurement for the cheeses is difficult unless you use a kitchen scale or buy exactly the amount of cheese you wish to use. But you can think of this recipe as creating a piece of art, edible of course, instead of exactly reproducing a scientific experiment.

Pasta with Four Cheeses

10 ounces spaghetti, cooked in about 4 quarts of boiling salted water
1 cup whipping cream
¼ cup parsley leaves, minced
1 large clove garlic, minced
1 ounce Parmesan cheese (½ to 1 cup freshly grated)
2 ounces Fontina cheese (about 1 cup cubed)
2 ounces cream cheese (4 tablespoons)
2 ounces Provolone cheese (about ¾ cup cubed)
Salt and pepper to taste.

Put the water on to boil while you begin doing the necessary mincing and chopping. When the water comes to a rolling boil, add the spaghetti and cook according to the instructions on the package.

Add the whipping cream to a large skillet and add the parsley, garlic, Parmesan, Fontina, cream and Provolone cheeses. Drain the pasta. Meanwhile heat the cream sauce over medium heat to melt the cheeses, stirring to insure complete melting and a smooth sauce. Add the well drained pasta to the sauce, toss to coat the pasta, and adjust seasonings if desired. Serve immediately on warmed plates if possible, because the pasta cools quickly. Serves four as a main course.

I BOUGHT A BEAUTIFUL head of Savoy cabbage at the Farmers' Market last week. I was so taken with its appearance that I gave little thought to what I would do with it once I got it home. I put the cabbage on the butcher block table in the middle of my kitchen and was pleased that a vegetable could be so visually satisfying. But then, since I am not an artist and could not use my magnificent vegetable as the centerpiece of a still-life painting, I decided that I would have to cook it.

I decided to make a Hungarian style dish that combines sautéed cabbage and egg noodles, seasoned with paprika and oregano, to serve with grilled pork chops. I think that a little sour cream could be stirred into the finished dish if you are feeling a bit decadent. The leftovers reheated very well.

Hungarian Cabbage and Noodles

1 package wide egg noodles (10 ounces)
¼ cup butter
1 medium onion, chopped
1 large head cabbage, finely chopped
1 teaspoon paprika
1 teaspoon oregano
¼ cup parsley, snipped (optional)
Salt and pepper

Boil the noodles following the directions on the package, taking care not to over-cook them. Drain the noodles and stir in a bit of the butter so that they will not stick together; then set them aside.

Sauté the onion in the remaining butter until it is golden brown. Add the cabbage to the skillet and continue cooking about 15 minutes, stirring often to prevent burning, until the cabbage is done to your liking. Stir in the paprika, oregano and parsley. Then stir in the noodles and add salt and pepper to taste.

Reheat if necessary and serve hot. Serves eight.

Sometimes it is necessary to plan ahead. For example, if you want to serve pasta with pesto sauce, grilled chicken and sliced tomatoes at an informal dinner party in late July, now is the time to plant the basil.

Some herbs are hearty enough to winter over in Minnesota. Tarragon, oregano and various types of chives do well. Plants bought at the greenhouse or donated by friends will signal the beginning of spring for many years to come. Other plants are more tender and need to be planted every year. Late each spring, I plant basil, two kinds of parsley, and rosemary. Technically, rosemary should winter over, but mine never seems to make it.

Basil is very much a warm weather plant. It likes warm ground in which to germinate and plenty of direct sun for growing. If your garden grows tomatoes, you should be able to grow basil. There are over 150 species of basil grown worldwide and almost every cuisine finds some use for this aromatic plant.

The varieties which seem to do best here are sweet basil, dark opal basil, and bush basil. If you plant the seeds in the garden or set out your plants in late May, by the end of July you should have plenty of basil for pesto, salads, and herbed vinegar.

Here is my pesto recipe. Pesto is a true peasant dish from northern Italy, and like all peasant foods there is no one correct way to make it. Use what you have on hand. Pine nuts are considered to be a traditional ingredient, but walnuts, almonds or even sunflower seeds may be used.

A good quality olive oil adds flavor and color and, of course, good cheese is always a plus. The pesto may be made with a mortar and pestle, a blender or a food processor. Pesto may also be stirred into mayonnaise, stuffed under the skin of chicken or added to your favorite vegetable soup just before serving. Pesto can also be frozen.

Pasta with Pesto

¼ cup pine nuts, walnuts or sunflower seeds (optional)
2 cloves garlic, peeled and lightly crushed
4 cups fresh basil leaves
½ to ¾ cup good olive oil
¾ cup Parmesan cheese, freshly grated
2 tablespoons softened butter
1 pound pasta

Finely chop the pine nuts in a food processor. Add the garlic while the processor is running. Add half of the basil and coarsely chop. Add the remaining basil and process to a medium chop. With the processor running slowly, add the olive oil and then the cheese and butter. Do not over process.

Cook the pasta al dente and add ½ cup of the hot pasta water to the pesto and process to just incorporate it. Drain the pasta and toss it with the thinned pesto in a large serving bowl. Serves four to six.

Salads & Salad Dressings

Carleton-Willis   Phampe

MEMORIAL DAY USHERS IN the picnic season. And with picnics comes the question of what to serve with the hamburgers, hot dogs or chicken. Here are two possible answers to that question. The first recipe is for a vegetable salad including potatoes, with a vinegar-oil dressing. The second recipe is for a lentil salad, which could also serve as a main course for vegetarians in the crowd.

Mushroom Vegetable Salad

¾ cup salad oil
½ cup wine vinegar
⅓ cup sliced green onions
¼ cup chopped parsley (optional)
2 teaspoons salt
1 ½ teaspoons sugar
1 teaspoon crushed oregano
¼ teaspoon pepper
4 cups potatoes cut into ½ inch chunks
1 pound fresh mushrooms
2 cups sliced zucchini
1 cup diced green pepper (optional)

Combine the oil, vinegar, green onions, parsley, salt, sugar, oregano and ground pepper; mix well.

Cook the potatoes in boiling salted water until tender, about 15 minutes. Drain the potatoes and place them in a large bowl. Stir the oil mixture and pour it over the potatoes. Mix gently and chill thoroughly.

Rinse, pat dry and slice the mushrooms. Add the mushrooms, zucchini and green peppers to the potatoes; toss lightly. Serves eight.

Lentil Salad

2 cups minced onion
2 tablespoons oil
1 pound lentils, washed and picked over
2 pound 3 ounce can plum tomatoes
1 cup oil
1 cup water
2 tablespoons minced garlic
1 teaspoon dried oregano
1 teaspoon dried basil
1 teaspoon dried thyme
1 bay leaf
3 tablespoons lemon juice
2 teaspoons minced garlic (optional)
Lemon juice, salt and pepper to taste

In a heavy saucepan, cook the onion in two tablespoons of oil until it's soft. Add the lentils, tomatoes (and their juice), oil, water, and the herbs and spices. Bring the liquid to a boil and cook the mixture covered, over low heat, stirring occasionally for one hour or until the lentils are tender and most of the liquid is absorbed.

Transfer the mixture to a non-metallic bowl, stir in the lemon juice, additional garlic, and salt and pepper to taste. Chill thoroughly.

Let the salad come to room temperature before serving, discard the bay leaf, and adjust the seasonings by adding additional salt, pepper and lemon juice if needed. Garnish with minced parsley and fresh tomato wedges if desired. Serves eight.

A GOOD POTATO SALAD goes well with grilled chicken, hamburgers or hot dogs, and it also doesn't contain all the additives that are found in packaged chips.

Many people like a cold potato salad, which is dressed with either mayonnaise or a boiled dressing, but I prefer a warm potato salad which has a bacon and vinegar dressing. I also think that new red potatoes, which are now available locally, make the best salad. I prefer to cook the potatoes with their skins on and then quickly peel and cut them into bite-sized pieces when they are still hot. While this salad is usually served warm, leftovers may be refrigerated and served later.

My grandmother's recipe for German potato salad was never written down, but here is a version which I think tastes good.

German Potato Salad

2 pounds red boiling potatoes
¼ pound bacon
1 tablespoon sugar
1 teaspoon flour
½ teaspoon dry mustard
5 tablespoons cider vinegar
5 tablespoons water
1 small onion, finely chopped
3 tablespoons parsley, minced
2 hard-boiled eggs, chopped
Salt and pepper to taste

In a large saucepan, cover the potatoes with water and cook them over medium heat until they can be pierced easily with the tip of a sharp knife; don't overcook them or the finished salad will be mushy. While the potatoes are cooking, fry the bacon until it is crisp and transfer it to a paper towel to drain. Pour off all but about two tablespoons of the bacon fat. Stir the sugar, flour and mustard into the fat and cook over a low heat for about 30 seconds. Add the vinegar and water and bring the mixture to a boil while stirring constantly.

When the potatoes are done, cool them until you can handle them and then peel quickly and cut them into bite-sized pieces. Pour the hot dressing over the potatoes. Crumble the bacon and add. Also carefully stir in the onion, parsley and egg. Taste for salt and pepper. Serve warm. Serves six.

THE FIRST LETTUCE FROM the garden always tastes special. It may be just a few leaves to put on a sandwich, or there might be enough for a small salad. But however much there is, it signifies that winter is truly over and there will be a summer of fresh produce to look forward to.

In general, I prefer homemade dressings to those bought in a bottle because they taste better and with a blender or food processor they are very easy to make. My favorite salad made from that first lettuce is dressed with a little balsamic vinegar and oil, seasoned with lots of freshly ground pepper and just a little salt and then topped with a generous portion of slivered Parmesan cheese.

Here is a recipe for a fresh herb dressing which is also excellent on a simple green salad or with vine-ripened tomatoes later on in the summer.

Fresh Herb Dressing

½ cup sour cream
½ cup mayonnaise
¼ cup chopped chives
2 tablespoons chopped tarragon
2 tablespoons chopped basil
¼ cup chopped parsley
2 tablespoons wine vinegar
1 teaspoon Worcestershire sauce
½ teaspoon prepared mustard
¼ teaspoon salt
⅛ teaspoon pepper
1 to 2 cloves garlic, peeled

Combine all the ingredients in a blender or food processor and process them until smooth. Store covered in the refrigerator. Makes about 1 ½ cups of dressing.

FRESH GARDEN LETTUCE IS certainly a welcome addition to the dinner table. Produce from California just can't compare with lettuce fresh from the garden in either taste or color.

Garden lettuce makes a superb Caesar salad. But sometimes it seems like too much bother to make one, or you may just want a small amount of salad. This bender Caesar salad dressing will keep for about a week in the refrigerator. It must come to room temperature before using or it will be too thick. If you use large cloves of garlic, it could also be used as a vampire repellent!

Blender Caesar Salad Dressing

1 pasteurized egg
½ cup grated Parmesan cheese
¼ cup lemon juice
1 or 2 cloves of garlic
1 teaspoon Worcestershire sauce
½ teaspoon salt
½ teaspoon pepper
½ cup salad oil

Place all the ingredients *except* the oil in a blender jar and blend them. With the motor running, slowly add the oil. Refrigerate for at least one hour to allow the flavors to blend. Allow the salad dressing to come to room temperature before using. Garnish the salad with croutons if desired.

THERE ARE PROBABLY MORE picnics on the Fourth of July than any other day of the year. In this part of the country, in addition to being the anniversary of our nation's founding, it also usually means that summer is really here. Here is a potato salad which will add nutrition and color to any picnic. Use new potatoes, as they hold their shape much better in a salad. Since this salad is dressed with oil and lemon juice instead of mayonnaise, it is safe to take on a picnic where refrigeration might not be available. Add the spinach just before serving.

Spinach-Potato Salad

⅓ cup oil
¼ cup grated Parmesan cheese
3 tablespoons lemon juice
2 teaspoons Worcestershire sauce
1 teaspoon salt, or to taste
Pepper to taste
4 cups warm, cooked sliced potatoes
3 cups shredded fresh spinach
2 to 3 hard-cooked eggs (to use as garnish)

In a large bowl, mix together the oil, cheese, lemon juice, Worcestershire sauce, salt and pepper. Add the potatoes and toss gently to coat them. Cover and chill well.

Before serving, gently mix in the spinach. Garnish with hard-cooked eggs cut into wedges. Serves four to six.

With the coming of hot weather, appetites can flag along with a cook's enthusiasm. A bottle of pop, a sandwich and some chips will supply the necessary calories and taste pretty good when served the first time, even though the combination may not be especially good for us.

It is almost as easy to serve a pasta or tuna salad with toast or garlic bread, along with homemade lemonade, which goes very well with salads and fresh fruit. This is especially appealing when most of the work can be done early in the day.

Here are the recipes for two salads with an Italian accent. The first is a traditional Italian white bean and tuna salad. A twenty ounce can of any type of white beans may be used in this recipe, thereby eliminating cooking altogether. Traditionally, oil-packed tuna is used, but substitute water-packed if that is what you prefer. It is also traditional to use red onion but Bermuda or chopped green onions may be used.

Tuna and Bean Salad

1 cup dried white beans
½ red onion, thinly sliced
1 seven ounce can good quality tuna, drained
⅓ cup olive oil
2–3 teaspoons red wine vinegar
Salt and pepper to taste

Cook the beans according to the package directions and drain (or drain and briefly rinse canned beans.) Place the beans in a salad bowl and add the onion. Add the tuna, breaking it into large flakes with a fork. Add the olive oil and vinegar, and salt and pepper to taste. Toss thoroughly and serve. Serves three to four.

The second recipe is for a pasta salad with cheese and pepperoni. The addition of a package or can of artichoke hearts would transform it into the gourmet class, but you can use 1–2 cups of whatever vegetable you prefer, such as thawed frozen peas, lightly steamed cauliflower or broccoli, or green beans. If you are on vacation, you can even use a prepared salad dressing.

Antipasto Pasta Salad

8 ounces uncooked small-shell macaroni
1–2 cups cooked vegetables
1 cup Italian salad dressing
2 green onions, sliced
2 cups cherry tomatoes, halved
2 ounces thinly-sliced pepperoni
1 cup (4 ounces) diced cheese

Cook the macaroni according to the package directions. Drain and cool it under running water and then drain thoroughly. In a large bowl combine the pasta, vegetables, salad dressing, green onions and cherry tomatoes. Cover and refrigerate at least 2 hours, stirring occasionally.

Before serving, cut the pepperoni slices in half and add them and the cheese to the salad. Toss. Serve on a large lettuce leaf, if desired. Serves four to eight.

IT HAS BEEN A long tradition in my family to have cinnamon toast and fresh fruit salad for a light supper when it is too muggy to think about spending time in the kitchen. The cinnamon toast is made by toasting good quality bread, buttering it while still warm and sprinkling it generously with cinnamon sugar. When enough toast has been made, the secret step takes place. The toast is put on a cookie sheet and placed under the broiler until the sugar begins to melt, transforming it into a special treat.

Here is the recipe for a spicy fruit salad which contains yogurt, raisins and nuts, as well as a mixture of whatever fresh fruit is currently available. The grated fresh ginger provides a pleasant bite.

If you do not have fresh ginger on hand, you can omit it, although if you have never used it, why not buy a small piece with which to experiment. Fresh ginger is also good for perking up stir fries. It will keep in the refrigerator for over a month when well wrapped.

Spicy Fresh Fruit Salad

1 ½ cups plain yogurt
2 tablespoons honey or ¼ cup sugar
½ teaspoon freshly-grated ginger
1 teaspoon cinnamon
¼ teaspoon nutmeg
¼ teaspoon ground cloves
6–7 cups mixed fresh fruit, cut in bite-sized pieces
½ cup chopped nuts (your favorite)
¼ cup raisins

In a large bowl, mix together the yogurt, honey or sugar, ginger, cinnamon, nutmeg and cloves. Gently fold in the fruit, nuts, and raisins. Chill before serving to five or six.

During our continued hot weather, the kitchen becomes an unpleasant place for many people. Cooking is hot work and appetites lag. A light supper of a tomato aspic salad with a creamy crab dressing, a crusty hard roll and a glass of chilled white wine, with cheese and fresh fruit for dessert will provide a cook's mini-vacation and some good eating. The same salad can be an excellent first course at a winter dinner party, or the aspic can appear on the table dressed with less exotic cottage cheese during the season when salad greens aren't up to par or too expensive.

Tomato Aspic

4 cups tomato juice
1 chopped onion
¼ cup chopped celery tops
2 tablespoons brown sugar
1 teaspoon salt
1 bay leaf
5 whole cloves
2 tablespoons (2 envelopes) unflavored gelatin
¼ cup cold water
3 tablespoons lemon juice

Combine the tomato juice, onion, celery, sugar, salt, bay leaf and cloves. Simmer for 10 minutes. Strain. Soften the gelatin in the cold water and add to the hot tomato mixture. Add lemon juice. Chill until firm in an eight inch cake pan or 1 ½ quart rind mold. Serve on a bed of lettuce with creamy crab dressing or seasoned cottage cheese. Serves four to six.

Creamy Crab Dressing

1 package or can (7 ½ ounces) crab meat
1 (3 ounce) package cream cheese
½ cup sour cream
2 tablespoons chopped onion, shallots or chives
3 tablespoons dry white wine
½ teaspoon garlic salt

Drain and flake the crab. Beat softened cream cheese with sour cream until smooth. Blend in the remaining ingredients. Chill. Makes two cups of dressing.

HERE ARE TWO SALAD recipes featuring mushrooms. The first is for a quick, fresh-tasting salad with green onions, sour cream and lemon juice. If you have fresh chives available, you might want to substitute about a quarter cup of freshly snipped chives for the green onion. The second would help you take advantage of the bounty of this year's bumper crop of zucchini, adding fresh carrots for contrast and extra nutrition, and a zippy mustard vinaigrette.

Fresh Mushroom Salad

1 green onion, minced
½ cup sour cream
3 tablespoons milk
1 teaspoon lemon juice
½ teaspoon salt
¼ teaspoon pepper
½ pound fresh mushrooms, thinly sliced

Mix together the onion, sour cream, milk, lemon juice, and salt and pepper. Gently fold in the sliced mushrooms. Serve in a lettuce cup if desired. Serves four to six.

Carrot, Zucchini and Mushroom Salad

4 large carrots, coarsely grated or cut into matchstick-sized pieces
½ pound mushrooms, thinly sliced
Dash of vinegar
4 medium zucchini, coarsely grated or cut into match-sized pieces
Mustard vinaigrette:
⅓ cup oil
2 tablespoons Dijon mustard
1 tablespoon wine vinegar
1 clove garlic, minced
1 teaspoon sugar
Salt and pepper

Blanch the carrots for 2 minutes in boiling salted water; drain well. Refresh them under cold running water and drain again. Blanch the mushrooms for 30 seconds in boiling water to which a little vinegar has been added; drain well.

Make the vinaigrette by combining all the ingredients in a small jar and shaking until they are emulsified. Extra vinaigrette may be kept in the refrigerator almost indefinitely.

Arrange the carrots, mushrooms, and zucchini and drizzle with the mustard vinaigrette to taste. Alternatively, the salad ingredients may be placed in a bowl and tossed with the dressing. Serves six.

As VEGETABLE GARDENS CONTINUE to produce, the novelty of having really fresh vegetables wears off, and you begin to wonder how to serve zucchini for the third time this week, how you can disguise the green beans, or what to do with the tomatoes that really should be eaten.

Last week when we went out to our favorite Minneapolis restaurant, we were served an excellent salad of coarsely shredded raw zucchini and carrots dressed with a vinaigrette sauce which was highly seasoned with freshly ground pepper. Another of my favorite salads is a combination of quartered tomatoes and thinly sliced onions (separated into rings) with this same vinaigrette, adding a little sugar.

Yet another good combination is green beans and tomatoes. My recipe for this week combines them in a Greek-style dish. When using fresh tomatoes in cooking, it is best to use only the pulp as the juice has little flavor and the skin and seeds harden when heated. To skin a tomato, drop it in boiling water for ten seconds, then cut out the stem and pull off the skin. To remove the seeds and juice, cut the tomato in half crosswise and gently squeeze, removing any seeds which stick with your fingertip.

Vinaigrette Sauce

½ to 2 tablespoons wine vinegar or a mixture of vinegar and lemon juice
6 tablespoons salad oil or olive oil
⅛ teaspoon salt
Pepper to taste

Place all ingredients in a screw top jar and shake vigorously to blend. Makes about ½ cup of sauce.

Green Beans with Tomatoes

1 pound cleaned green beans
¼ cup oil
1 cup pealed, chopped tomatoes
½ cup chopped onion
1 teaspoon red wine vinegar
½ teaspoon dried oregano
½ teaspoon marjoram

Cook the green beans, drain and keep them warm. Heat the oil over moderate heat in a medium-sized skillet. Add the remaining ingredients and simmer covered for five minutes. Add the beans and simmer uncovered an additional five minutes. Season to taste with salt and pepper. This recipe may also be made with frozen beans and Italian-style plum tomatoes. Serves four.

ORANGES AND TANGERINES ARE in good supply at the supermarkets right now, and by no means should this bounty be restricted to appearing in a glass at breakfast time or fitting into the corner of a brown bag carried to school or work.

The addition of orange slices or sections to a green salad adds both eye and taste appeal. If you also add a few thin onion rings to your salad and use orange and lemon juice in the dressing, you have a truly excellent salad to be eaten with either a simple casserole or a gourmet dinner.

The combination goes especially well with fowl or fish dishes or with Mexican food. Since there is no vinegar in the dressing, the salad can even be eaten as you sip a glass of wine, provided the wine isn't too sweet.

Orange and Onion Salad

Salad:
2 oranges
2 medium, mild onions
Mixed salad greens (spinach is especially good)

Dressing:
½ cup oil
½ cup orange juice
2 tablespoons lemon juice
Pinch of rosemary
1 teaspoon salt

Peel the oranges and cut them into sections or thin slices, removing all the white inner peel which tends to be bitter. Peel and slice the onions very thin, separating them into rings. Wash and dry the greens, breaking them into bite-sized pieces. Blend the oil, juices and seasonings and combine them with the oranges and onions in a large bowl. When ready to serve, add the crisped greens and toss well. The proportions of greens, onions and oranges can easily be changed to suit individual preferences, or the number being served.

If you are looking for a change in the green salad you put on the table, you might try making it using fresh spinach instead of lettuce. You can also make a tasty salad by grating raw carrots and dressing them with a little lemon juice, freshly ground pepper and salt to taste. Tomato aspic also makes a good salad when topped with a simple dressing made of avocado, along with lemon juice to keep the avocado from changing color, a little minced garlic, and salt and pepper.

I had one of the best salads I have ever eaten at a restaurant in Long Beach, Calif. recently. We looked at the Queen Mary through the restaurant's picture windows. When we got home, I decided to recreate it. Here are the results.

California Spinach Salad

8 slices bacon (about one-third pound)
10 cups spinach (one 12 ounce package)
Salt and pepper to taste
¼ cup lemon juice
2 tablespoons white wine vinegar
1 teaspoon Dijon mustard
1 ½ tablespoons sugar
1 egg
Hard-cooked egg for garnish

Cook the bacon until crisp, drain on a paper towel, cool it to room temperature, and crumble it into a large salad bowl. Remove the stems from the spinach, wash it, pat dry, and tear the spinach into bite-sized pieces, adding them to the bacon. Sprinkle with salt and pepper to taste and toss.

Combine the lemon juice, vinegar, mustard and sugar in a small saucepan, mixing well. Heat the mixture to the boiling point and then reduce heat to low. Beat the egg in a small bowl. Gradually add half of the lemon mixture to warm the egg. Pour the entire egg mixture back into the saucepan and cook, stirring briskly until thickened, about 3 minutes. Do not allow to boil.

Pour the hot dressing over the spinach, toss gently to coat it and garnish with chopped hard-cooked egg. Serve immediately. Serves eight.

If I were to choose my favorite city among those we recently visited in northern Italy, I would choose Florence. It is a bustling, busy city where the shop windows are adorned with tomorrow's fashions and the squares with art treasures, which in other cities would be tucked away in museums. You are apt to find a statue that your book mentions standing just where it has stood since the Renaissance with no plaque to tell you what it is.

Not that Florence doesn't also have more than it's share of museums. The Uffizi Gallery, which houses the treasures that the Medici family accumulated during the three centuries they ruled the city, is one of the great art galleries of the world. The works of Botticelli, Dürer, Raphael, da Vinci, Michelangelo, and many others fill room after room. It is impossible to absorb them all in one visit. There are also the Pitti Palace, the Bargello Museum, the Medici Chapels, and the Academy Gallery, where Michelangelo's "David" is displayed.

But the art is only part of the city for me. I usually don't enjoy shopping, but the windows displayed such a wealth of leather goods, beautiful paper, gold of fine workmanship, brightly colored clothes, and even yard goods, that it was fun to wander along looking.

The farmers' market inspired me to use a whole roll of film in an attempt to capture the variety of truly fresh produce displayed with the artistic splash that the city seems to inspire — raspberries in small leaf-lined baskets with each berry perfect, tomatoes arranged according to size, mounds of polished eggplants.

And then there was the lovely food we ate. It was plain in the sense that there were not a lot of fancy sauces, but the variety was great. We ate mostly at places which specialized in traditional regional foods. Most meals began with a selection of cold antipasti — things like thin slices of eggplant and zucchini, which had been brushed with oil and broiled, fresh anchovies, marinated artichokes and sweet onions, quiche-like tarts made with bread, eggs, zucchini and onions, and assorted olives. This was followed by soup or pasta and then the main course. The meat was often roasted or grilled. The vegetables were often served with oil and vinegar to be added according to the diner's liking. The salads contained fresh mushrooms and thin slices of Parmesan cheese with lettuces that were bitter to my taste. All of this was accompanied by varieties of hearty Tuscan bread and by wine from the vines which grow around the city. Finally, if you still had room, there was dessert, which was often cheese or fresh fruit.

Here is a recipe for a Tuscan bread salad, which I watched being made in the kitchen of our favorite Florentine restaurant. The bread used in this salad must be of good quality, a firm whole wheat loaf, or else the salad will be too mushy. I used Brownberry wheat bread when working out the quantities.

Natale Bread Salad

4 slices slightly stale whole wheat bread
2 medium tomatoes, diced
1 small cucumber, diced
½ large white onion, diced
5 tablespoons olive oil
2 tablespoons red wine vinegar
1 teaspoon oregano
5–8 drops Tabasco or other hot pepper sauce to taste
Salt and pepper to taste

Soak the bread in ice water for about 10 minutes and then squeeze as much moisture as possible from it. Crumble the bread into a medium-sized bowl. Dice the tomatoes, cucumber, and onion into about half inch pieces and add them to the bread.

In a small bowl mix together the olive oil, vinegar, oregano, hot pepper sauce, and salt and pepper. Pour this over the bread mixture and toss. Refrigerate the bread salad for several hours before serving. Serve at room temperature. Serves six.

I WON'T HAVE ANY leftover turkey to use up this year because we are spending the holiday week with our vegetarian children in Seattle. In fact, since we will be in Canada on Nov. 28, we probably won't celebrate Thanksgiving. The Canadians have their harvest holiday in September.

But I know that many of you will have lots of turkey left. After you have made sandwiches, creamed it and made your favorite hot dish, you might want to turn the thermostat up a couple of degrees, pretend that it really isn't winter and serve a fruited turkey pasta salad. This salad would also make an interesting addition to a holiday potluck. Vegetarians could leave out the meat altogether, and still have a very tasty salad.

For ease in making, a bottled Italian dressing may be used or you can substitute your own favorite oil and vinegar dressing. If you want to splurge, use fresh pineapple; canned pineapple tastes good too, even though the salad will be a bit sweeter. Chicken may be used instead of turkey. Hot muffins go well with the salad.

Turkey Pasta Salad with Fruit

Salad:
8 ounces curly noodles
2 big oranges, peeled and sectioned
2 cups pineapple cubes
1 cup seedless grapes, halved if desired
2–3 cups cubed, cooked turkey

Dressing:
½ cup Italian dressing
½ cup orange juice
½ to 1 teaspoon grated orange rind
2 teaspoons honey

Cook the noodles according to the directions on the package, being careful not to overcook; drain and rinse with cold water, then drain well and place in a large bowl. Add the oranges, pineapple, grapes and turkey and stir to mix.

Make the dressing by combining the Italian dressing, the orange juice and rind, and the honey. Pour the dressing over the salad and refrigerate it for at least an hour, so that the pasta will absorb some of the dressing. Serve on lettuce leaves and garnish with roasted almonds or sliced, unpeeled red apple. Serves four to six.

Sauces & Seasonings

Scoville · Carleton   PhampE

Recently, an ad in the *Minneapolis Tribune* caught my eye. It was for a Twin Cities chain of grocery stores and simply listed the thirty-five fresh vegetables they had for sale. The best thing about the list was that almost all of the items are available at one or another of our Northfield grocery stores. Times have changed from when winter vegetables meant canned peas, beans, corn or tomatoes, with perhaps a few carrots or rutabagas and an occasional squash, which had been stored in a root cellar. Now, besides the many frozen vegetables, almost any vegetable is available fresh at the supermarket all year around.

The important thing to remember about cooking any fresh vegetable, winter or summer, is not to overcook it, so that you destroy much of the vegetable's nutritive value and end up with a mushy, tasteless product. All a well cooked vegetable really needs is the addition of a little butter and salt and pepper before appearing on the table. A small squeeze of lemon juice added to the melted butter is nice especially with green vegetables. But the popularity of sauced frozen vegetables testifies to the fact that many people prefer their veggies disguised or at least dressed up a little.

Here are the recipes for two sauces which go well with vegetables. The cheese sauce is especially good with cauliflower, broccoli or green beans. Hollandaise is traditional with artichokes and goes well with almost any green vegetable except peas. Both sauces will keep for several days in the refrigerator.

Cheese Sauce

3 tablespoons butter or margarine
4 tablespoons flour
3 cups milk
1 ½ cups grated Cheddar cheese
Salt and pepper

Melt the butter in a heavy saucepan over low heat. Add the flour and cook for about two minutes, stirring constantly. Gradually add the milk, again stirring constantly. Bring the mixture to a boil, reduce the heat and simmer gently for 10 minutes, stirring occasionally. Add the cheese and continue simmering until it is completely melted. Season to taste with salt and pepper.

You might like to further season the sauce with a little (¼ teaspoon) nutmeg or a couple of dashes of Worcestershire sauce. Makes about 3 ½ cups of sauce.

Blender Hollandaise Sauce

Yolks of 4 pasteurized eggs
2 tablespoons lemon juice
½ teaspoon salt
⅛ teaspoon red pepper (optional)
½ cup butter, melted

Place all ingredients except the butter in a blender jar. Turn the blender on and off quickly. Heat the butter until it is hot and bubbly. Turn the blender on high and dribble the hot butter steadily into the egg mixture. The sauce will emulsify and thicken. Makes about one cup of Hollandaise sauce.

I'M A FIRM BELIEVER in gravy and am always surprised when people say they can't make it. I usually don't recommend products by brand name but if you use Wondra instant-blending flour, you will find that making gravy is a snap.

Easy Pan Gravy

For each cup of gravy desired, use the following:

2 tablespoons meat drippings
2 tablespoons Wondra flour
1 cup cold water, milk or broth (or any combination of the three)
Salt and pepper to taste

Remove the meat from the pan to a platter that has been warmed. Pour the drippings from the pan, leaving any brown bits behind. Skim excess fat from the drippings and measure the desired amount of drippings back into the pan. Sprinkle the flour over the drippings and stir in the liquid. Heat to boiling over medium heat while stirring constantly and scraping any brown bits from the bottom of the pan. Boil and stir for about one minute. Add salt and pepper to taste.

These recipes for making seasoning blends at home can be used to stock your kitchen, as well as for unusual Christmas gifts. Co-ops are excellent sources of fresh, bulk spices. You can buy just the amount you need.

All-Purpose Seasoning Blend

¼ cup hot Hungarian paprika
½ teaspoon dried basil
¼ teaspoon cayenne (red) pepper
¼ teaspoon dried marjoram
¼ teaspoon dried thyme
⅛ teaspoon ground black pepper

Mix all ingredients together and store in an airtight container away from the light. Use for casseroles, chicken, fish and salad dressings.

Italian Seasoning

1 tablespoon dried marjoram
1 tablespoon dried basil
2 teaspoons dried thyme
1 teaspoon dried rosemary, crumbled
1 teaspoon dried savory
½ teaspoon dried sage
1 teaspoon dried oregano

Combine all ingredients thoroughly and store in an airtight container away from the light. Use to season meat, vegetables, casseroles and salads.

Herbes de Provence

1 tablespoon dried thyme
1 tablespoon dried oregano
1 tablespoon dried marjoram
1 tablespoon dried savory
½ bay leaf, crumbled

Mix the herbs together thoroughly and store in an airtight container away from the light. Use in soups, stews and casseroles.

Seasoned Pepper

1 tablespoon white peppercorns
1 tablespoon black peppercorns
½ teaspoon Sechuan peppercorns
6 whole coriander seeds
4 whole allspice

Put all ingredients in a peppermill or electric blender and pulverize to a coarse powder. Store in an airtight container away from the light. Use wherever you would use black pepper.

One of the things that have made American cuisine so much fun in the last few years is the freedom to borrow, adapt and combine foods of many different origins. It is enjoyable to eat or prepare a classic French or Italian dinner, which presents a challenge to both the cook and the palate of the eater. But it is also fun to be able to serve vichyssoise and hamburgers or Caesar salad and hot dogs and discover that they taste good together.

Another change in American cuisine has been the switch of taste from sweet to sour and from bland to spicy. The change hasn't been a sweeping one, but experimentation is taking place in many kitchens.

One type of recipe I have had several requests for is chutney. One book defines chutney as an Indian relish, cooked or un-cooked, of fruit, vegetables and spices mixed together and served with curries and cold meats. However, this definition does not mention that ginger is the traditional spice used in chutneys.

Recipes for chutneys appeared in some very early American cookbooks. They were brought to the shores of New England by sailors engaged in the India trade, and thrifty housewives recognized that the pungent preserves could cover the taste of food which was suffering from lack of refrigeration. When it became possible to keep food fresher for a longer time, the popularity of strong tasting condiments, except for ketchup and mustard, waned in this country.

Since the end of World War II, American interest in food, its preparation and taste, has grown. The preparation of ethnic meals for guests has led to the use of some ethnic foods on everyday tables, as well. Chutney, like any condiment, has the advantage of letting the eater choose how much to use. However, the cook may also want to try adding a bit of chutney to the dressing used on a chicken or tuna salad or even a fruit salad.

Here is a recipe for rhubarb chutney. If you use green or fresh ginger, remember to fish the pieces out before serving because it can be quite a shock to your taste buds to bite into a piece of raw ginger. The chutney would go well with pork, grilled chicken or any poultry. This recipe is easy to halve.

Rhubarb Chutney

2 pounds fresh rhubarb, cut into 1 inch pieces (about 8–9 cups)
2 cups brown sugar, lightly packed
1 ½ cups chopped onion
1 cup cider vinegar
½ cup dried currants or raisins
2 teaspoons curry powder
1 teaspoon ground ginger or 3–5 thin slices fresh ginger, bruised with the flat of a knife
1 teaspoon salt (if desired)

Combine all the ingredients in a large saucepan; do not use a non-coated aluminum pan, as the acids in the chutney can react with aluminum, turning it dark. Heat the mixture to a boil, stirring it often. Reduce the heat and continue cooking for about 50–60 minutes, stirring to prevent sticking, until the chutney becomes thickened. Spoon it into sterilized jars and seal. It can be stored in the refrigerator for up to three months. Makes about four cups.

When we hosted a large holiday buffet dinner recently, smoked turkey was one of the entrees. With the turkey, I served a cranberry-lime chutney, which was a fresh, tart-tasting contrast to the rich, smoky taste of the meat. This chutney would be good with any smoked meat, poultry or pork. Since it is now possible to obtain frozen cranberries all year long, I decided not to save this recipe for a holiday column. The chutney is just too good for only one or two annual appearances.

Cranberry-Lime Chutney

1 large orange
1 tart apple
2 cups cranberries
2 ⅔ cup brown sugar
1 tablespoon grated lime zest
3 tablespoons lime juice
½ cup cider vinegar
¼ cup water
¼ teaspoon nutmeg
⅛ teaspoon ginger
⅛ teaspoon dry mustard
¼ teaspoon allspice

Peel the orange, remove any white membrane clinging to the fruit, and cut the orange into quarter inch slices. Peel, core and coarsely chop the apple. Wash and pick over the cranberries. Place the fruit and all the remaining ingredients in a large non-aluminum saucepan. Stir to mix. Place the pan over high heat and bring to a boil. Reduce the heat to low and simmer for 45 minutes, stirring occasionally. Serve warm or at room temperature. Makes two cups of chutney.

WE RECENTLY WENT OUT to dinner with friends to celebrate our February birthdays and had a truly memorable dinner, cooked to perfection. In general it is difficult to duplicate the results that a fine restaurant obtains because many of the ingredients they pay premium prices for are just not available to the general public.

However, there was one dish we had that can be duplicated quite easily and deliciously at home. For an appetizer I had fresh California asparagus with Maltaise sauce, which is similar to Hollandaise sauce, except that it is made with orange juice rather than lemon juice and the sauce is further seasoned with grated orange peel. The restaurant made Maltaise sauce in the traditional way, using blood oranges grown on the island of Malta. I made the sauce using California oranges and it was still lovely. The finished dish was garnished with very thin strips of orange zest, the brightly colored portion of the orange peel.

Maltaise sauce is my favorite topping for fresh asparagus; remember not to overcook the asparagus. The sauce would also be good with broccoli or artichokes.

Maltaise Sauce

2 pasteurized egg yolks
1 tablespoon fresh orange juice
2 teaspoons grated orange peel
6 tablespoons butter
White pepper and salt
Orange zest and halved orange slices for garnish

Combine the pasteurized egg yolks, orange juice and grated orange peel in a blender container and whirl until well mixed. Heat the butter in a small pan until it is bubbly. With the blender running, slowly pour the hot butter into the egg yolk mixture. Season to taste with salt and pepper. Spoon the sauce over cooked asparagus and garnish with threads of zest and orange slices.

Soups

Popcorn Wagon   PLAMPE

There seems to be a bumper crop of morels this year. For the uninitiated, morels (*Morchella esculenta*) are edible spring mushrooms, which appear in wooded areas after abundant rainfall. Their very characteristic pitted cap has led Clyde M. Christensen of the University of Minnesota to classify them among his foolproof four, those mushrooms which anyone should be able to identify. They are one of Minnesota's choicest eating mushrooms.

If you collectors would like to make something different with part of your harvest, you might try making a German-style mushroom and potato soup, which is delicious when made with morels. I used one 10½ ounce can of beef broth diluted with two cans of water for the stock. Remember, the quantities given are suggestions, not absolutes.

Wild Mushroom and Potato Soup

¼ pound bacon, finely chopped
1 medium onion, thinly sliced
1 pound wild mushrooms, cleaned and halved
2–3 medium potatoes, cubed
1 quart stock or water
Salt and pepper

In a large, heavy saucepan, fry the bacon until it's crisp and then add the onion and cook for about three minutes. Add the mushrooms and cook an additional five minutes. Add the potato cubes and stock (or water) and simmer for approximately 45 minutes. Season to taste with salt and pepper. Each bowl of soup may be garnished with a little sour cream.

Recently, we went out to dinner with friends and had a truly memorable meal. One dish that I had, Greek lemon soup, can be duplicated quite easily and deliciously at home. Remember that the eggs are stirred into the hot broth just before serving. You *cannot* reheat this soup.

Greek Lemon Soup

3 cups chicken broth
½ cup cooked rice
2 eggs
2 to 3 tablespoons lemon juice

Heat the broth and rice to boiling in a large saucepan. Beat together the eggs and lemon juice until the mixture is thoroughly combined and uniform in color.

Remove the broth from the heat and stir about a quarter cup of the hot broth into the egg mixture to gradually warm it. Then slowly add the egg mixture to the hot soup, stirring constantly. Serve immediately. Serves four.

A CHICKEN AND SAUSAGE gumbo makes a good one-dish supper on a blustery March evening. In Louisiana they use a French sausage called andouille in their gumbo. You may not find this at the meat counter of a local market, but any smoked, fully-cooked, beef sausage would be an acceptable substitute.

A gumbo owes its unique color and flavor to a roux which is made with flour and the oil or fat in which the chicken and sausage have been browned. This mixture is then cooked until it becomes a deep mahogany brown and smells as if the flour were beginning to burn. Care must be taken not to let the flour actually scorch, however, or the whole dish will taste burnt. If you are not cooking in a heavy cast-iron pan, you might want to do this step in a non-stick skillet. The browning process can be done as quickly and over as hot a fire as you are comfortable using. It destroys 90–95% of the gluten in the flour, so that the resulting soup is not thickened by the flour.

Just a word about three ingredients which appear in all Creole cooking: onions, celery and green peppers. They are so basic to this type of cooking that they are often called the trinity. They appear in the proportion of two cups of onion to each cup of celery and green pepper.

File is a word often associated with gumbo. File powder is made by finely grinding the young leaves of the sassafras tree. When the powder is mixed with a hot liquid, it has certain thickening powers as well as a unique taste, which some people like while others don't; if file is cooked, it becomes stringy and unattractive. If you don't have any file powder or don't like it, try finishing each dish of gumbo with about a tablespoon of good sherry.

Chicken and Sausage Gumbo

1 cup oil
1 chicken, 3–4 pounds, cut up
1 ½ pounds smoked beef sausage, sliced
1 cup flour
4 cups onions, coarsely chopped
2 cups celery, sliced
2 cups green pepper, chopped
1 tablespoon garlic, minced
8 cups stock or water with bouillon
Cayenne pepper to taste
Salt
1 cup green onions, chopped
1 cup parsley, minced
File powder, if desired
Cooked rice

In a large pot, sauté the chicken until it is golden brown and then remove it from the pan. Brown the sausage in the same oil and then set it aside. Make a roux by adding flour to the oil and cooking until it's a deep, fragrant brown. Add the onions, celery, green pepper and garlic to the hot flour mixture and continue cooking over low heat until the vegetables are just tender. Return the chicken and sausage to the pan. Gradually stir in the stock and bring to a boil. Reduce to simmer and cook for at least an hour. Season to taste with cayenne pepper and salt. About 10 minutes before serving add the green onions and parsley. Serve over rice. Add ¼–½ teaspoon of file powder or a tablespoon of sherry to each serving if desired. Serves eight generously.

Black bean soup is one of my favorites. It is also a good way of utilizing leftovers from a traditional Easter dinner. The bone and scraps from the ham go into the soup and the extra hard-cooked eggs provide the garnish, which is traditional with this soup.

Black beans, or turtle beans as they are sometimes called, are one of the traditional beans of Caribbean cooking, but they are also popular in Western and Mexican cooking in this country. They have a very smooth texture and distinctive flavor when cooked. This recipe calls for Madeira wine, but sherry may be substituted, or the wine may be omitted altogether.

Black Bean Soup

1 pound black beans
8 cups water
5 strips bacon, cut in small pieces
3 large onions, chopped
2 stalks celery, chopped
2 tablespoons flour
Ham bone or 2 ham hocks, split
2 10 ½ ounce cans beef broth
2 bay leaves
2 cloves garlic, crushed
2 carrots, chopped
¾ cup Madeira
Salt and pepper to taste
Hard cooked eggs, chopped
Very thin lemon slices

Wash the beans, cover them with cold water and soak overnight. Drain the beans and rinse again.

Place the beans in a large pan or Dutch oven, cover them with eight cups of water, cover the pan and simmer for about 90 minutes. Cook the bacon in a heavy skillet until the fat is rendered, add the onion and celery and cook until tender. Add the flour and cook, stirring, for about a minute; add about one cup of liquid from the beans, stir thoroughly, and then add this mixture to the remainder of the beans and liquid. Add the ham bone, beef broth, bay leaves, garlic and carrots to the pot. Cover and simmer over low heat, stirring occasionally, for four hours. Add more water if the soup becomes too thick.

Remove the bones and meat from the soup. Purée the soup through a coarse sieve or food mill. Chop the meat fine and return it to the puréed soup.

Reheat the soup. Add the Madeira and adjust the seasonings to taste. Garnish each serving with finely chopped hard-cooked egg and a thin slice of lemon. Serves eight generously.

With the weather we have been having lately, one hesitates to say spring is here even though the calendar says so. Years of living in Minnesota have taught me that spring will indeed come; in fact, some years it comes several times before it decides to stay.

Spring brings a change in activities. It always seems to be an extra busy time at our house, when I am not inclined to spend more time in the kitchen than I have to. It is a time when it is especially nice to have something in the freezer that can be prepared quickly (read thawed).

Here is a recipe for a basic bean soup, which can be frozen in appropriate portions and then gussied up so that no one will suspect that it is the same basic soup you have been serving for the past month. The soup recipe serves six generously and is easy to double. The garnishes are designed to be stirred into a whole recipe of soup but they can easily be halved if you are serving a smaller quantity.

You can use your own taste to govern the amount of "goodies" you add; the garnishes are just suggestions. Create your own soup du jour. Any favorite kind of beans—navy, great northern, pea, pinto or even soybeans can be used. Double-strength reconstituted nonfat dry milk can be substituted for the whole milk the recipe calls for.

Basic Bean Soup

6 cups cold water
2 cups dried beans
¼ cup oil
1 large onion, chopped
1 large carrot, sliced
1 stalk celery, chopped
1 teaspoon soy sauce
2 cups whole milk
2 egg yolks
½ cup whipping or sour cream
Salt and pepper to taste

Combine the water with washed and picked over beans in a large pan and let them soak at least eight hours. In a small pan, sauté the onion, carrot and celery in the oil until the vegetables are soft, but not browned. Add the vegetable mixture and soy sauce to the soaked, undrained beans, adding more water if necessary to cover the beans by about one inch of liquid. Bring to a boil, cover and simmer over low heat for about 1 ½ hours or until the beans are tender. Transfer the mixture, in batches, to a processor or blender and purée; then return it to the pan.

Combine the milk, egg yolks and cream in a small bowl and add about ½ cup of the warm soup mixture. Add the egg mixture to the soup, stir well, and then add salt and pepper to taste. Heat the soup, but do not boil it. Serve as is or add the desired garnish. The soup may also be served cold. The ungarnished soup freezes well.

Suggested Garnishes

Tomato and chives:

2 medium tomatoes
¼ cup finely-chopped chives

Peel, seed and chop the tomatoes. Add the tomatoes and chives to the hot soup and stir gently to mix. Check for seasoning and serve.

Mushroom and green onion:

1 tablespoon oil
1 teaspoon lemon juice
1 cup finely-chopped mushrooms
½ cup chopped green onions

Heat the oil and lemon juice in a small skillet. Add the mushrooms and sauté them for about 1 minute. Stir in the green onions and add the mixture to the hot soup. Stir, taste for seasoning, and serve.

Curry and toasted nuts:

2 teaspoons curry powder or to taste
¼ cup fresh parsley, finely chopped
1 cup toasted almonds or peanuts, finely chopped

Stir the curry powder into the hot soup. Place over low heat and cook, without boiling, for 3–4 minutes, stirring constantly. Remove from the heat and stir in the nuts and parsley. Serve.

Spinach and cheese:

1 cup finely-chopped fresh spinach
½ cup grated Parmesan cheese

Stir the spinach into the hot soup and serve. Add the cheese separately at the table.

On a recent rainy Saturday, I attended a Mexican cooking class. It was in a home that is a treasure house of Mexican pottery, wrought iron and cut tin. The table was decorated with a large tin bowl of spring flowers and two magnificent cut-tin roosters with glittering blue eyes.

I must admit that I approached this class with some trepidation. I had not had much experience with Mexican food, but I know that I do not like very highly spiced or "hot" food, and I do not eat green peppers, which in my ignorance I had equated with any pepper that was green. I found to my surprise that a properly prepared chili need not remove the lining of your mouth, and that chilies taste nothing like green peppers.

Here is the recipe for a fresh asparagus soup that we ate.

Sopa de Esparragos

(Mexican Asparagus Soup)

2 cups chopped, cooked asparagus
4 cups chicken broth
¼ to ½ cup of peeled, seeded green chilies, chopped
Salt and pepper to taste
1 cup sour cream

Heat the asparagus, chicken broth and chilies together for about 10 minutes to blend the flavors. Purée in a blender or food processor. Add salt and pepper to taste. Ladle into soup dishes and serve with a generous dollop of sour cream, which tames the hotness of the chilies. Serves six.

If you have a well-producing asparagus patch, you might be starting to wonder what to do with your bounty. Usually, asparagus cooked until it is just crisp and tender is a fit dish for any table whether it is topped with your favorite sauce or just a bit of butter. But if you have already served it four times this week, you might want to try something different.

Cream of Asparagus Soup

1 pound asparagus
1 onion, thinly sliced
1 ½ cups chicken broth
2 tablespoons butter
2 tablespoons flour
1 cup light cream or whole milk
Salt and pepper to taste

Cook the asparagus in a small amount of water until it is just barely tender. Drain and reserve the cooking water. Cut off the asparagus tips and set them aside.

To the asparagus water, add the asparagus stalks, onion and chicken broth. Boil for five minutes and then purée in a blender or rub through a sieve.

In a large sauce pan melt the butter and stir in the flour. Stir in the puréed soup and cook, stirring constantly for 5 minutes. Add the cream or milk and salt and pepper.

Before serving it, gently reheat the soup to serving temperature. It may also be served well chilled and garnished with finely chopped, hard-cooked egg. Place the asparagus tips in the soup plates and pour the soup over them. Serves six.

Over the Fourth of July weekend we attended "Taste of Minnesota," which was held on the grounds of the state capitol. Luckily we went on Saturday, thereby avoiding the storms of Sunday and the crowds on the Fourth. We had a good time strolling among the thirty food booths and choosing our meal for the utmost variety and so that our tickets came out even.

I had a little trouble convincing my husband that marinated strawberries topped with cream could serve as our salad, but other than that we put together a varied and tasty sampling of what the various Minnesota restaurants had to offer. Of course, we couldn't try everything, but by sharing each purchase we did get to sample the wares of eight booths. Our meal began with a chilled pear, peas and watercress soup and ended with a delicious black raspberry Italian ice.

The soups reminded me of what a nice beginning a chilled soup is to a meal when the weather is warm. My Scandinavian heritage makes me somewhat partial to fruit soups, but vegetable ones are good too.

Melon Soup

⅔ cup sugar
2 ½ cups water
2 pounds melon (cantaloupe, Crenshaw or casaba), seeded and peeled
1 cup dry white wine
Lemon juice to taste
½ to 1 cup sour cream
Nutmeg

Place the sugar and water in a medium-sized saucepan, stir until the sugar is almost dissolved, and then bring to a boil over medium heat. Boil for three to four minutes and cool; chill as needed. Purée the melon and wine in a food processor or blender. Add the sugar syrup and lemon juice to taste. Add the desired amount of sour cream and blend again. Chill until serving time. Top each serving with a sprinkling of freshly grated nutmeg. Serves six.

Gazpacho

4 cups cold tomato juice
1 small onion, finely minced
2 cups diced fresh tomatoes
1 green pepper, minced
1 cucumber, diced or thinly sliced
2 green onions, sliced
¼ cup fresh parsley, chopped
1 clove garlic, crushed
Juice of ½ lemon
Juice of 1 lime
2 tablespoons wine vinegar
2 tablespoons olive oil
1 teaspoon basil
1 teaspoon tarragon
Dash of Tabasco sauce
Salt and pepper to taste

Combine all ingredients and chill thoroughly (at least two hours) before serving. Serves six to eight.

TOMATOES WERE ORIGINALLY GROWN as a decorative plant. Since the tomato plant is a member of the nightshade family, it was long thought that the fruit was too poisonous to eat. But after some brave souls ate them and lived to tell about it, recipes began appearing for tomato preserves and then for the use of tomatoes in salads and sauces. It is difficult to imagine what Italian cuisine or even the American favorite, the hamburger, would be like today if the unknown hero hadn't taken that first bite.

It's getting to be that time of the season when the wonder of the taste of garden-ripened tomatoes is beginning to be dulled by the question, "Can I possibly put a plate of sliced tomatoes on the table again tonight?" If you have already sliced them, stuffed them, broiled and baked them, scalloped, stewed, and sautéed them, here is a recipe for a delicious fresh-tasting cream of tomato soup.

Cream of Tomato Soup

2 tablespoons butter
1 tablespoon oil, preferably olive oil
1¼ cups thinly-sliced onion
3 large ripe tomatoes, coarsely chopped
3 tablespoons tomato paste
4 tablespoons flour
2 cans chicken broth (10 ½ ounce size)
1 teaspoon sugar
Salt and pepper to taste
1 cup heavy cream
2 tablespoons butter

In a large saucepan, heat two tablespoons of butter with the oil and sauté the onion for about five minutes. Stir in the tomatoes and tomato paste and cook for another two or three minutes. Sprinkle the mixture with the flour and mix well. Add the chicken broth, sugar, and salt and pepper. Simmer for 15 minutes. Pour into a blender and blend at high speed for several seconds. Strain through a fine sieve. Return the soup to the saucepan and add the cream. Bring to a boil and then reduce the heat and simmer for two to three minutes. Before serving, stir in the remaining butter, bit by bit. Serves six to eight.

THE FARMERS' MARKET IS an absolute delight to the senses this harvest season. When I went last week, I bought some of the most beautiful leeks I have seen, raspberries that were so juice-filled that they looked ready to burst, shallots of generous size and beautiful purplish-brown color, and apples polished until they glowed. Carrots, beets, onions, potatoes, squash in all sizes and shapes, pumpkins, melons of several varieties, cucumbers, tomatoes both yellow and red, beans, and even strawberries tempted one to buy more and more and more.

One can't help but wonder what someone from the world's poorer countries would think of the variety and bounty. Perhaps we should revive the old custom of harvest festivals and celebrate our own Thanksgiving at this bountiful time of the year.

Leeks are a sentimental favorite of mine. One scene I will always treasure is that of a very little girl, apron clad, standing on a stool in front of a washbowl full of water with French whisk in hand, stirring the water with great concentration. When asked what she was making, she replied with the gravity which a three-year-old can attain when doing something really important. Her answer consisted of one word: "Veeshee-swahz."

I think most of us have a favorite food that is especially comforting to us—that sustains us with both nourishment and memories. My daughter Sara decided at a very early age that leek and potato soup or vichyssoise was her personal favorite. It sustained her through the normal childhood illnesses, teething, strep throat and new braces.

Sara and her father disagree on how the soup should be served. Sara prefers hers hot while Jerry likes his well chilled and served with a sprinkling of chives and an extra grinding of pepper. Technically, Sara likes leek and potato soup while her father eats vichyssoise which *is* served cold.

One thing about leeks is that they are difficult to clean. When they are growing, the dirt is hilled up around them so that they remain white. This means that there is usually dirt in between the layers of the leek. The easiest way to clean a leek is to cut off the roots and the heavy dark green tops. This will leave you with a piece six to ten inches long. Quarter this lengthwise, spread the layers apart, and rinse out the dirt and grit under running water. Discard the tough dark green part of the leaves but use the tender light green portion of the inner leaves.

Vichyssoise
(Leek and Potato Soup)

3–4 leeks, white and pale green part, sliced
4 tablespoons butter
5–6 medium-sized potatoes, peeled and cubed
2 quarts chicken broth
2 cups light cream (half-and-half)
Salt and pepper to taste
Chives for garnish (optional)

In a large pan, cook the leeks in the butter until limp. Add the potatoes and the chicken broth. Simmer partially covered for 35 to 40 minutes or until the vegetables are very tender. Pass the soup through a food mill or purée it in batches in a blender. Stir in the cream. Season to taste. Serve either warm or well chilled. Garnish with chives.

When days turn cooler, I am ready to sing with Lewis Carroll's Mock Turtle, "Soup of the evening, beautiful soup!" And one of the most beautiful soups, in my opinion, is onion soup topped with French bread wearing a crown of melted Swiss cheese.

With the addition of a salad, perhaps a glass of wine left over from the making of the soup, and light dessert you have a meal that you can be proud to serve to your favorite people.

You can make a reasonable soup by browning your onions in a little butter and then adding them to your broth. But to get the most flavor from the onions, they should have a long, slow cooking in butter and oil so almost all of the moisture is cooked out of them. They then need a long simmering with the stock to blend the flavors. This recipe takes about 2½ hours from start to finish.

The recipe calls for a cup of wine. This may be left out but the flavor will be different. When wine is used in cooking, it is added early enough in the process so that all the alcohol is gone by the time the dish is finished, leaving the flavor of the wine but not the taste of the alcohol.

This recipe makes lots of soup. I usually serve it once when freshly made and then freeze the remainder in containers which hold two servings each.

Onion Soup

3 pounds thinly-sliced yellow onions (about 10 cups)
6 tablespoons butter
2 tablespoons oil
2 teaspoons salt
1 teaspoon sugar
6 tablespoons flour
4 quarts beef stock (6 cans beef bouillon diluted with an equal amount of water)
1 cup dry white wine
Toasted French bread and grated Swiss cheese for garnishing

Cook the onions slowly in the butter and oil for 15 minutes in a large (6 quarts or more) covered pan. Uncover, add the salt and sugar to help the onions brown, raise heat slightly, and cook for 30 or 40 minutes, stirring frequently to prevent burning. The onions should be an even golden brown.

Sprinkle in the flour; stir and cook for five minutes. Stir in the beef stock and bring to a boil. Add the wine and season to taste with salt and pepper. Simmer for at least 30 minutes, skimming if necessary.

To serve, place the hot soup in an oven-proof bowl, add a thick slice of toasted French bread, top with grated Swiss cheese and place under a hot broiler until the cheese melts. This recipe makes twelve generous servings. The soup freezes well.

As the weather turns cooler, soups begin to play a more important part in my menu planning. A couple of weeks ago a friend asked me if I had a recipe for a carrot soup, and I had to admit that I didn't. In fact, I had never even considered making carrot soup. Carrots are something you always find in a good vegetable soup or you might find flecks of carrot in a bean or lentil soup or even in chicken soup with rice, but a soup featuring just carrots?

But you know how it is sometimes. An idea presents itself and you can't get it out of your mind until you do something about it. Here is a recipe for a very attractive carrot soup, which could be served either hot or cold—although I think it tastes better hot. If you serve the soup hot, you might want to try topping each serving with about a quarter cup of grated cheddar cheese. If you are serving it cold, a dollop of sour cream, plain yogurt, or a sprinkling of chives would make an attractive garnish.

Cream of Carrot Soup for Laudie

4–5 large carrots (about 1 ¼ pounds)
1 large onion, sliced
3 cups chicken broth
¼ teaspoon ground white pepper
1 teaspoon ground ginger
1 cup light cream
Nutmeg (optional)

Peel the carrots and slice them about ¼ inch thick. In a large saucepan combine the carrots, onion and chicken broth. Bring to a boil, cover and simmer until the carrots are tender (about 10 minutes). Pour half the mixture into a blender and purée it. Repeat with the other half. Return the soup to the saucepan and add the pepper, ginger and cream. The soup may be refrigerated at this point.

Stir the soup over low heat until it is hot. Pour it into bowls and garnish with a little freshly-grated nutmeg, if desired. Serves four.

THE DAMP, COLD WEATHER we have been having lately seems to call for a bowl of good, hot homemade soup. Somehow soup seems to help dispel the chill which is apt to settle in one's soul when the sun doesn't make its appearance for days on end, when the tomatoes freeze before you get around to picking them, when the yard is covered with wet, soggy leaves, and when you feel as though you might be getting a cold.

Most people have their own favorite soup for these occasions, but if you would like to try something different, here is a recipe for squash bisque which is quite tasty. Served with a bit of cheese, some warm crusty bread and some polished apples, it could make a complete meal.

Like most soup recipes, this one is very adaptable. Use your favorite type of winter squash. You can even use two packages of frozen squash if that is what you like. The chicken broth can be of the canned variety. You can use a cup of half-and-half instead of a half cup of whipping cream and a half cup of milk. Or if you are watching calories, just use milk. It is a forgiving recipe.

Squash Bisque

3 tablespoons butter
1 cup chopped onion
¼ cup diced carrots
2 medium potatoes, peeled and cubed
4 cups chicken broth
3 to 3 ½ cups peeled, cubed squash
½ cup whipping cream
½ cup milk
Salt and pepper to taste
Dash of red pepper (optional)

Melt the butter in a large saucepan. Add the onion and carrots and cook covered over low heat for about 10 minutes or until the vegetables are tender. Add the potatoes, chicken broth and squash and simmer covered over low heat for about 25 minutes or until the vegetables are very tender. Force the mixture through a sieve or whirl it in a blender until it is smooth. Return the puréed mixture to the sauce pan and add the cream and milk. Salt and pepper to taste. Reheat the soup just before serving. Sprinkle each bowl of soup with red pepper if desired. Serves six to eight.

When the icy wind is howling outside, there is something especially satisfying about sitting down to dinner and having a good bowl of home-made soup. If the soup is accompanied by a piece of hearty bread and perhaps a bit of cheese, you have a simple and delicious meal. The recipe I am going to share with you takes a little planning ahead, but I think the results are worth the effort.

This bean soup recipe can easily be doubled or even tripled. I once made it using ten cups of beans and twenty quarts of water for a church supper. This soup comes close to reproducing the famous U.S. Senate bean soup.

Bean Soup

1 cup navy or marrow beans
8 cups water
A small piece of ham, ham bone or ¼ pound salt pork
1 bay leaf
8 peppercorns
6 cloves
2 diced carrots
6 stalks celery, chopped
1 chopped onion
2 minced cloves of garlic
1 cup mashed potatoes

Wash and pick over the beans. Soak in cold water overnight and then drain. In a large kettle bring the eight cups of water to a boil. Add the beans, meat and spices. Cook the soup slowly until the beans are almost tender, about 2½ hours. Sauté the carrots, celery, onion and garlic in a small amount of oil for five minutes, add to the soup and continue cooking for a half hour. Add the mashed potatoes (instant will do). Remove and mince the meat. Put the soup through a food mill or sieve. If the soup is too thick, thin it with water or milk. Correct the seasoning and stir in the meat. The soup serves four generously and freezes well.

What to serve for Saturday night supper often seems to be a problem. Quite often the day has been a busy one, doing all the things you hadn't gotten around to doing the rest of the week. A bowl of home-made soup, a salad and a piece of good bread make a satisfactory end to a busy day.

Cheddar ale soup is easy to make. For something different, garnish the bowls of soup with popcorn or crumbled crisp bacon. Rye bread goes particularly well with this soup. It does not freeze well, but the recipe can easily be cut in half.

Cheddar Ale Soup

½ cup butter or margarine
⅓ cup minced onion
⅓ cup grated carrot
½ cup flour
¼ teaspoon dry mustard
½ teaspoon paprika
3 cans chicken broth
¼ pound grated Cheddar cheese (2 cups)
1 cup half and half
1 twelve ounce can ale or beer

Melt the butter in a large heavy saucepan. Add the onion and carrot; cover and cook over low heat about five minutes. Blend in the flour, mustard and paprika. Stir in one can of the chicken broth. Add the cheese and cook over medium heat, stirring constantly, until the cheese is melted. Add the remaining ingredients and simmer for 30 minutes, stirring occasionally. Makes seven cups of soup.

Here is a recipe for a tomato-cheddar cheese soup that takes only about a half hour to make and have ready for the table.

Tomato-Cheddar Cheese Soup

1 medium onion, finely chopped
¼ cup butter or margarine
1 can (29 ounces) tomato purée
2 ½ cups water
10 ounces extra-sharp cheddar cheese, shredded
Salt to taste
1 cup sour cream

In a large sauce pan sauté the onion in the butter until it is soft. Stir in the tomato purée, water and cheese. Gently heat, stirring fairly often, until the cheese melts. Do not allow the soup to boil, which may cause it to curdle. Taste for seasoning. Stir about 1 cup of the soup into the sour cream in a small bowl and then stir the cream mixture back into the remaining soup. Serves six (makes two quarts of soup).

Soup served at the beginning of a meal should be light and flavorful, setting the tone for the meal to come. If your main course is a simple grilled steak, chop or chicken, you might want to serve a slightly richer creamed soup. If your main dish is heavily sauced or has lots of gravy, a simple vegetable soup might be better.

The secret of this soup is making sure your vegetables are really thinly sliced. Canned chicken broth may be used, and you can dilute the soup before serving it, if necessary.

Potato Vegetable Soup

4 medium potatoes, peeled, thinly sliced
1 small onion, thinly sliced
2 medium carrots, thinly sliced
½ teaspoon thyme
½ teaspoon marjoram
4 cups chicken broth
4 cups water
Salt and pepper to taste
2 cups thinly-sliced zucchini
Grated Parmesan cheese

Combine the potatoes, onion, carrots, thyme, marjoram, broth and water in a large saucepan. Bring to a boil and season with salt and pepper. Simmer, covered, until the vegetables are just tender (about 15 minutes). Stir in the zucchini and cook an additional 2 or 3 minutes. Serve topped with grated cheese. Serves eight.

So far, we have had a comparatively mild winter, but I'm going to be prepared for the worst by having the makings for several pots of home-made soup ready for the coming week.

The first recipe is for a simple mushroom soup. If you thought all mushroom soup came in cans, you are in for a pleasant surprise. You may use canned chicken broth in this recipe, however. The soup would be good before any simple meal. It could be served with a hamburger or alongside that all-time American favorite, the grilled cheese sandwich.

The second recipe is for a hearty Scandinavian fish chowder that needs only the addition of a good crusty piece of bread to make a meal. This recipe can also be made with left-over fish.

I serve one of my favorite winter desserts, sliced oranges, after each soup. The orange slice may be sprinkled with a little orange liqueur or topped with a dusting of coconut.

Mushroom Soup

½ pound fresh mushrooms, sliced
2 tablespoons butter or margarine
2 tablespoons flour
2 cups light cream (half-and-half)
2 cups chicken broth
1 egg yolk
1 tablespoon lemon juice
Salt and pepper to taste

In a large saucepan sauté the mushrooms in the butter until barely tender, about 3 minutes. Stir in the flour and cook until bubbly. Slowly stir in the cream and chicken broth. Reduce the heat, cover the pan and simmer for about 10 minutes.

Beat the egg yolk and lemon juice together and stir in some of the hot soup. Then add the egg mixture to rest of the soup, mixing well. Do not let the soup boil after the egg is added. Taste for seasoning and serve immediately. Serves four.

Scandinavian Fish Chowder

3 cups water
3 potatoes, peeled and cubed
3 green onions with tops, sliced
¾ pound boneless fish, cubed
¾ cup heavy cream
2 tablespoons flour
1 tablespoon butter
Salt and pepper

In a large saucepan, bring the water, potatoes and onions to a boil. Reduce the heat and simmer until the potatoes are just tender, about 20 minutes. Gently stir in the fish and simmer five minutes. Mix together the cream and flour and add to the soup, stirring gently. Cover the soup and simmer an additional five minutes or until the soup is slightly thickened and the fish is done. Stir in the butter and taste for seasoning. Serves four.

Visiting vegetarians can present a problem to meat-eating hosts who want to respect their guests' preferences but also know that their own family feels somewhat deprived when meat doesn't appear on the dinner table. I recently solved this problem by serving a very hearty lentil soup with lots of good bread, followed by spinach and fresh orange salad garnished with toasted sunflower seeds and a good selection of cheeses with more bread. I also served custard and cookies for dessert. Everything tasted good and I don't think that anyone went away from the table unsatisfied.

Remember that a recipe for soup leaves room for creativity. I do not think that I have ever made any soup exactly the same way twice. Here is my latest version of lentil soup.

Lentil Soup

2 cups lentils (1 pound)
6 cups water
1 ½ teaspoons salt
1 tablespoon minced garlic
1 cup chopped onion
½ cup minced celery
½ cup chopped carrot
Pepper to taste (lots)
1 can (28 ounces) whole tomatoes in juice
Juice of 1 lemon
2 tablespoons brown sugar
1 teaspoon oregano
1 teaspoon basil

Wash and pick over the lentils. Put the lentils, water and salt in a large pan and simmer, covered, for 2–3 hours, until the lentils are tender. In a large frying pan using a little oil, sauté the garlic, onion, celery and carrot until tender but not browned; add this to the lentils and continue simmering. Add the desired amount of pepper. Cut the tomatoes into small pieces and add them along with their juice to the lentils. Stir in the lemon juice, brown sugar, basil and/or oregano. Simmer at least another 30 minutes before serving. Serves eight generously. Freezes well.

Vegetables

Also see...

St Olaf - Steensland

Phampe

Daffodils, pussy willows and asparagus—SPRING! Since the first two are edible only if you are a rabbit, I will concentrate on the third.

The first domesticated asparagus in the United States was probably grown by early Dutch settlers. This would have been green asparagus transplanted into their gardens from nearby woods. Over the next three hundred years, more than twenty varieties of asparagus were cultivated, including white asparagus with pink or purple tips.

The white asparagus is still the most popular in Europe, where the serving of the first spring stalks is almost a mystical experience for some people. I think the fresh pungent flavor of our green crop is the equal of the white asparagus I have eaten in Europe.

I prefer to buy slender stalks which are green all the way to the bottom and have firm, compact tips. If the stalks are limp, they aren't very fresh. When I get my asparagus home, I break off the woody ends and stand the stalks up in a jar of water like a bouquet before placing the jar in the refrigerator. In this manner you can keep your asparagus reasonably fresh for up to four or five days. I have never found it necessary to peel the stalks unless they are very thick.

The important thing to remember is not to overcook asparagus. When overcooked it becomes olive green and mushy. It probably doesn't have much food value then either.

The easiest way to cook asparagus is to steam it. Place a single layer of stalks in a steamer basket above a couple of inches of boiling water and cook until the asparagus shows only a slight resistance to the tip of a sharp knife.

You may also boil your asparagus. I place mine in a bread pan, adding boiling water to cover and cooking briskly until just barely tender, and then draining it immediately.

You can also cook your asparagus upright in a tall double boiler or percolator. Tie the stalks into serving sized bunches and place them in a coffee pot. Add boiling water to come halfway up the stems and cook them until the tops show little resistance to a sharp knife point. In this way, the tougher bottoms are boiled while the tender tops are steamed. When cooking asparagus, start testing for doneness after five minutes. Cooking time can vary between five and 15 minutes. You may wish to cook your asparagus, drain it, and then cool it under running water to stop the cooking and set the color. When ready to serve, you can re-heat it briefly either in a little butter or hot water.

When you tire of eating just plain asparagus, try topping it with browned butter which has a little lemon juice added to it, or Hollandaise sauce, or a simple cheese sauce.

Asparagus also goes well with poached eggs as a brunch or luncheon dish. The soft yolk ends up acting as a sauce.

Asparagus and Poached Eggs

3 tablespoons butter
3 shallots minced or 2 tablespoons minced green onions
2–3 pounds thin asparagus, trimmed and cooked
4 eggs, poached until whites are firm but yolks are still soft
Salt and pepper

Melt the butter in a large skillet. Add the shallots and cook briefly. Add the cooked asparagus and sauté only until heated through. Divide the asparagus among four heated plates and top each serving with a freshly poached egg. Sprinkle with salt and pepper and serve immediately with hot buttered toast. Serves four.

Now is the time to visit the Farmers' Market. It is a wonderful experience to be able to choose from such abundance. When I went last week, I bought both strawberries and raspberries, corn, eggplant, zucchini, and some tiny new red potatoes. Tomatoes, beans, cucumbers, onions, melons, apples, all kinds of potatoes, herbs, carrots, beets, eggs and even fresh lima beans were available. There were pickles and jellies, baked goods, including homemade pies, and some lovely quilted potholders. There also seem to be more flowers this year. An unadvertised benefit of the Farmers' Market is that I always seem to meet someone I haven't seen in a while. It is pleasant to stand in the warm sunshine and visit for a few minutes.

Our vegetarian son is home for a visit, so the eggplant was turned into meatless moussaka, which turned out quite well but made more than we needed. The eggplant was very large. The recipe could easily be cut in half and baked in an eight inch square pan. It is possible to heat up the leftovers, but I don't think this dish would freeze very well. Use fresh basil if available.

Meatless Moussaka

1 large eggplant (1 pound)
5 tablespoons oil
1 large onion, finely chopped
1–2 cloves garlic, minced
4 large tomatoes, chopped
1 carrot, shredded
½–1 teaspoon basil
Pepper to taste
½ teaspoon cinnamon
¼ cup minced parsley
1 cup frozen peas (optional)
2 cups cooked brown rice
½ cup chopped walnuts

Custard:
2 tablespoons butter
2 tablespoons flour
1 ½ cups milk
Pepper to taste
⅛ teaspoon nutmeg
1 cup ricotta cheese
2 eggs, well beaten
¼ cup grated Parmesan cheese

Peel and slice the eggplant into ½ inch slices. Place the slices in a lightly oiled 9×13 pan and drizzle 3 tablespoons of oil over them. Bake in a preheated 400° oven for 15 minutes.

Meanwhile, heat the remaining oil in a large frying pan and add the onion and garlic; fry until the onion is limp. Add the tomatoes, carrot, basil, pepper, cinnamon, parsley and peas and set aside.

Spread the rice over the eggplant slices and spoon the tomato mixture over the rice. Sprinkle the walnuts over the top. At this point the dish may be refrigerated until about 1 hour before serving time.

Make the custard by melting the butter in a small saucepan and stirring in the flour. Add the milk gradually and cook, stirring constantly, until thickened (about 10 minutes). Remove from the heat and add the pepper, nutmeg and ricotta cheese and stir well. Add the eggs, mix well, and then stir in the Parmesan cheese. Pour the custard over the casserole and bake in a preheated 350° oven for 45 minutes. Let stand for a few minutes before serving. Serves eight.

The first European explorers of the New World brought a small yellow fruit home to Europe with them. The Italians called it pomo d'oro or apple of gold and adopted it wholeheartedly. This seedy little fruit was the ancestor of our modern tomato, which is now gracing our gardens and markets in such abundance.

Over the centuries Italian horticulturists were responsible for breeding the small yellow tomato into its present form: large, red and meaty. In the rest of Europe, tomatoes were only slowly accepted because many feared that they were poisonous like some of their cousins in the nightshade family. Others ate them with gusto because of the tomato's reported aphrodisiac powers, and the French even called them pommes d'amour or love apples. We now know that they are neither poisonous nor an aphrodisiac, and we eat them because they taste good and are a good source of Vitamin C. In fact, today they are eaten in quantities which make them second only to the potato in vegetable popularity.

Late in the 19th century the Supreme Court of the United States officially decided that the tomato is a vegetable and not a fruit. The word fruit originally meant any plant used as food, but gradually it came to mean the edible layer which surrounds the seeds of a plant. Eighteenth century botanists formalized this meaning; anatomy defined if a plant was a fruit or a vegetable. The word vegetable also came to mean a plant food eaten along with meat or other parts of a meal. This means that while anatomically green beans, eggplant, cucumbers and corn are fruit, we commonly call them vegetables based on culinary custom.

The Supreme Court case came about when a New York food importer claimed duty-free status for a shipment of tomatoes from the West Indies because they were fruit and, according to the regulations of the time, not subject to import fees. The customs agent disagreed and imposed a ten percent duty on the shipment he defined as vegetables. Since the Constitution offered no guidance in the matter, the court decided on the grounds of linguistic custom. The majority of the court held that tomatoes are "usually served at dinner in, with, or after the soup, fish, or meat which constitutes the principal part of the repast, and not, like fruits, generally as dessert." This officially made the tomato a vegetable and the importer had to pay the duty.

Here is a recipe for cheese stuffed tomatoes which go particularly well with steak or chops. Use about 1 ½ teaspoons of minced fresh basil instead of the dried, if you have it available.

Cheese Stuffed Tomatoes

3 large tomatoes, halved
¼ cup soft bread crumbs
1 tablespoon butter, melted
½ teaspoon dried basil
Salt and pepper to taste
½ cup grated Monterey Jack cheese
1 tablespoon chopped parsley

Scoop out the center of each tomato half, leaving a ½ inch thick shell, and place the tomatoes in a shallow baking pan. Chop the scooped out tomato pulp and set it aside.

In a medium-sized bowl, combine the bread crumbs, butter, basil and salt and pepper. Stir in the cheese and chopped tomato pulp. Fill the tomatoes with the cheese-bread crumb mixture and bake in a preheated 350° oven for about 10 minutes or until the cheese melts. Sprinkle with parsley before serving. Serves six.

I HAVE REALLY ENJOYED going to the Farmers' Market the last couple of weeks. The weather has been lovely, the produce top quality, and the people friendly. Two of my favorite fall crops, leeks and shallots, have been available along with all sorts of tomatoes, squash, cucumbers, melons, beans, onions, potatoes, carrots, lettuces, eggplants and the last of the corn and raspberries. Many people seem surprised with the amount that they purchase. Last week I bought apples, potatoes and a couple of melons, as well as leeks, lettuces and eggs. It took me two trips to carry the bounty to my car.

Another nice thing about the Farmers' Market is that you get to pick out exactly what you want. I enjoyed watching one woman pick out three perfectly matched tomatoes. They would have been perfect for baking, filled with cheese soufflé.

Since eggs come in indivisible units, it is sometimes difficult to get the soufflé mixture to come out even with the number of tomatoes you are using. The cheese mixture in this recipe could be piled into three or four large tomatoes to be served as an entrée, or in up to eight medium-sized tomatoes if you wanted to serve them as an appetizer or a vegetable to accompany a meat dish. If you are very patient, it could even be stuffed into innumerable cherry tomatoes for use as hors d'oeuvres.

The herbs used to season the soufflé can suit your own preference. Basil is always good with tomatoes or fresh chives would be pretty. If you are using fresh herbs, you will need at least a teaspoonful instead of the half teaspoon called for in the recipe. I have had good luck in freezing fresh herbs by washing and carefully drying them before placing them on a cookie sheet in the freezer. When they are frozen, I place them in plastic bags, which allows me to remove small amounts as I want them.

Soufflé Stuffed Tomatoes

4 to 8 ripe tomatoes
½ teaspoon salt
4 tablespoons butter or margarine
1 ½ tablespoons flour
½ cup milk
3–6 drops hot pepper sauce
¾ cup grated Cheddar cheese (about 3 ounces)
½ teaspoon dried basil, oregano or tarragon
3 eggs, separated

Cut a ½ inch slice off the stem end of each tomato and scoop out the pulp, which may be saved for another use or discarded. Salt the insides of the tomatoes and invert them on several thicknesses of paper towel to drain for about an hour.

Melt the butter in a medium-sized saucepan and blend in the flour. Add the milk and cook, stirring constantly, over medium heat until the sauce boils and is smooth. Remove from the heat and stir in the pepper sauce, cheese and your choice of herbs. Beat in the egg yolks, one at a time.

Beat the egg whites until stiff and add about one fourth of the whites to the cheese mixture, mixing thoroughly to lighten it. Then carefully fold in the remaining egg whites. Spoon the soufflé mixture into the prepared tomatoes and mound the tops. Place the tomatoes in a buttered baking dish and bake for 25–30 minutes in a preheated 375° oven. The tops of the tomatoes will be puffed and golden brown when done.

RATATOUILLE IS A VEGETABLE stew from the Provence region in southern France. It is also one of the treats of harvest cooking here in Minnesota. All of the good things which go into ratatouille are now in abundance in our gardens or at the Farmers' Market: eggplant, zucchini, onions, garlic, tomatoes and green peppers. The proportions of vegetables may vary greatly and, in fact, probably the only really essential ingredients are eggplant, garlic and tomatoes. If I have an abundance of green beans, I add them, and I also use other kinds of summer squash than zucchini.

Ratatouille is a very versatile dish. It may be served either hot or at room temperature. It can fill the role of appetizer, salad, vegetable or condiment. Vegetarians might like to serve it over pasta or atop brown rice or kasha with a healthy sprinkling of grated cheese. It reheats and freezes well. I always make several large batches and freeze meal-sized portions for winter enjoyment. It can be cooked on top of the stove or, if you are making a large batch, simmered in the oven.

Remember this recipe is just a guide. Use your imagination to please your own individual taste. For example, if you really like hot foods, experiment by adding some red pepper or hot sauce; if you love garlic, add some extra; if you hate green peppers, leave them out.

Ratatouille

2 tablespoons olive oil
2 cloves garlic, crushed
1 large onion, thinly sliced
1 medium eggplant, cubed
2 medium green peppers, diced
4 large tomatoes
3 medium zucchini, sliced
2 teaspoons dried basil
1 teaspoon dried oregano
½ teaspoon dried thyme
2 tablespoons parsley
Salt and lots of pepper to taste

Heat the olive oil in a large pot which has a lid. Add the garlic and onion and cook until soft, about seven minutes. Add the eggplant and stir to coat it with oil. Add the green pepper and stir well. Cover the pot and cook over medium heat for about 10 minutes, stirring occasionally to prevent sticking. Add the tomatoes, zucchini and herbs; mix the ratatouille well. Cover and cook it over low heat for about 20 minutes. The zucchini and eggplant should be soft but not mushy. Taste and add salt and pepper, if desired. Serve hot or cold. Serves four to six.

It seems strange that so many of the maples are already beginning to turn scarlet while vegetable gardens are just getting their second, or in some cases their first wind after the rains of the last two weeks have finally brought new life. It is certainly nice to go to the Farmers' Market and see so much fresh produce.

Cold marinated vegetables make a pleasant change from the steamed or stir-fried vegetables which usually appear on the table. Here is a recipe for a colorful combination of lightly cooked cauliflower and zucchini with cherry tomatoes, which can be served as is for a Greek-style side dish, tossed with lettuce for a green salad, or used in a vegetarian pasta dish. Use one tablespoon minced fresh basil instead of the dried if you have it available.

Marinated Garden Vegetables

1 medium cauliflower (1 pound)
4 medium zucchini (1 ¼ pound)
1 cup cherry tomatoes, halved
½ cup chopped green pepper (optional)
¾ cup white wine vinegar
½ cup oil
¼ cup sugar
1 teaspoon dried basil
Salt and pepper to taste

Cut the cauliflower into small flowerets. Cook it in a large covered saucepan for six to eight minutes in a small amount of boiling water. Halve and slice the zucchini. Add it to the cauliflower and cook an additional four to six minutes. The vegetables should be crisp-tender. Drain.

In a bowl combine the cooked vegetables, cherry tomatoes and green pepper. In a screw-top jar combine the vinegar, oil, sugar, basil and salt and pepper. Cover the jar and shake well to combine the ingredients. Pour this marinade over the vegetables. Cover and refrigerate overnight or for up to three days. Makes eight cups.

Lettuce Toss: Tear one small head of lettuce into bite-sized pieces. Toss with four cups of the vegetable mixture and ¼ cup of the marinade. Serves eight.

Vegetable Pasta Salad: Cook eight ounces of noodles or fettucini in a large amount of boiling salted water until the pasta is just tender. Drain and rinse with cold water until the pasta is chilled. Toss the pasta with four cups of the drained vegetable mixture and ¼ cup of the marinade. Sprinkle with ¼ cup grated Parmesan cheese. Serves six to eight.

THE CRANBERRY SHRUB IS an American plant. Native Americans used the bright red berries in making pemmican in which dried meat and mashed cranberries were bound together with fat. This high-energy food was particularly useful when Indians were on the move. They also recognized the medicinal value of the berry, which we now know has a high Vitamin C content.

The Native Americans introduced use of the berries to the Pilgrims, who gave the berry its name. Someone thought that the delicate pink blossoms of the bush looked like cranes' heads, and so the berries became cranes' berries, which turned into cranberries. The Pilgrims probably ate the berries that first Thanksgiving Day. Soon the colonists began exporting cranberries. They became a staple on clipper ships, helping to prevent the dreaded scurvy.

Cranberries were first cultivated on Cape Cod. Today they are grown commercially in Massachusetts, New Jersey, Wisconsin, Oregon, Washington and on Canada's Pacific coast. When buying fresh cranberries, look for berries that are plump, firm and shiny. You should be aware that most cranberries are now marketed in twelve ounce packages so you may have to adjust your favorite recipes to the lesser amount or buy additional packages of the fruit. The berries can be kept for up to a month in the refrigerator and for up to a year in the freezer. Discard any soft or discolored fruit before using.

Acorn squash and cranberries has become one of my favorite wintertime vegetable dishes. It goes very well with turkey, chicken or pork. You can easily increase or decrease this recipe by remembering to use equal amounts of cranberries and brown sugar. You might also want to try adding a little nutmeg along with the cinnamon.

Acorn Squash and Cranberries

2 acorn squash
1 cup cranberries
1 cup brown sugar
1 teaspoon cinnamon
2 tablespoons butter

Cut the squash in half lengthwise, remove the seeds, and place in a shallow baking pan. Combine the cranberries, brown sugar, and cinnamon and divide the mixture between the pieces of the squash. Dot with butter. Cover loosely with foil and bake in a 350° oven until tender, about 1 ¼ hours. Serves four.

When American restaurants specialize in ethnic food, what they serve is often quite different from what is served in the food's native land. There are several reasons for this, a major one being that it is often difficult, and sometimes impossible, to obtain all the necessary ingredients here. This means that the menu must either be limited or adjustments must be made in the preparation of some dishes.

Another reason is that some restaurateurs feel that the American palate is unadventuresome and will not try anything that is too "foreign." Therefore, they compromise themselves into a blandness which can be disappointing if you go expecting "the real thing."

Since we returned from Italy last summer, we have eaten in several Italian restaurants hoping to recapture the delightful dining experiences we had there. Italian food doesn't call for too many exotic ingredients, but it does demand fresh ones if it is to be authentic. In a few restaurants that is what we got. The herbs used were fresh, the olive oil fine, the cheeses of good quality, the veal exquisite, the pasta not overcooked.

In one of our recent forays, I had carpaccio (thinly-sliced raw beef served with flakes of Parmesan cheese, olive oil and lemon juice), pasta with four cheeses, veal sautéed with porcini mushrooms and white wine, and an excellent serving of spinach sautéed with roasted garlic and butter. With the good bread that was served and a bottle of hearty Italian red wine, it provided a most pleasant finish to what had been a rather trying day.

Here is my version of spinach with roasted garlic. By the way, roasted garlic spread on fresh toast with goat cheese and a little chutney makes a delicious appetizer. Roasted garlic may also be used in any recipe calling for the addition of garlic or as a vegetable with a roast. You will be surprised at the mellow taste the garlic has when prepared in this way.

Roasted Garlic

10–12 large cloves garlic, peeled
2 tablespoons butter
2 tablespoons oil
Salt and pepper to taste

Heat the butter and oil together in a small casserole. Add the peeled garlic and turn so that each clove is coated with the butter mixture. Bake in a preheated 350° oven for 25 minutes, basting occasionally. Add salt and pepper.

Sautéed Spinach with Roasted Garlic

1 ½ to 2 pounds fresh spinach
3–4 tablespoons butter
2–6 cloves roasted garlic
Salt

Thoroughly wash the spinach, discarding any leaves that are not crisp and green and removing any tough stems. Make sure all the sand and grit is removed. Place the wet spinach in a covered pan and cook over medium heat for 6–10 minutes, until just tender. Drain well. All this can be done ahead of time.

Melt the butter in a skillet and add the desired amount of roasted garlic, mashing it coarsely with a fork. Add the spinach and sauté for two minutes or until hot. Add salt if desired. Serve hot. Serves four to six.

Afterword

The recipes in Tastes Good use ingredients that are locally available, and fresh, seasonal foods are the recurring theme. Beyond the Northfield Farmers' Market and the local supermarkets two other places may be especially useful for your food purchases. The first is Lorence's Strawberries, which also sells fresh asparagus and raspberries, and the second is the Just Food Northfield Community Co-op.

Index

JEAN SCHWOLOW MOHRIG was born in
1936 in Chicago and grew up in Elmhurst,
Illinois. She attended Carleton College in
Northfield, graduating with a major in
chemistry. Jean and Jerry met in graduate
school at the University of Colorado and
married in 1960. They moved to Northfield in 1967 when Jerry joined the faculty
at Carleton. Jean was a creative and devoted mother who took
great delight in raising her three children, and she was a friend to
many members of the Northfield community. Her cooking skills
were well known locally and were a joy to her family, the guests
at her table, and the readers of "Tastes Good" in the *Northfield
News*.

After her son Jonathan died in 1984, Jean returned to school at
the United Theological Seminary of the Twin Cities where she
completed her Master's Degree. She remained connected to the
seminary, serving as a member of the Alumni Board. Jean was an
active member of the United Church of Christ, Northfield. She
also studied feminist theology at the Episcopal Divinity School
in Cambridge, Massachusetts, and was committed to the Re-
Imagining movement.

Jean was an avid reader and among her many volunteer efforts
she was a member of the Board of the Northfield Public Library
and one of its staunchest supporters. She loved to travel; the
North Shore of Lake Superior and Italy were favorite destina-
tions. Jean died unexpectedly in an accident in 1999 while on a
nature walk near Lake Superior.